CONFERRING WITH THE UNIVERSE

How energy guidance protects and shows me the way

S. SCOTT UNDERWOOD

Published by: Tom Bird Retreats, Inc.

E-MAIL: sscottunderwood@gmail.com

WEBSITE: sscottunderwood.com

Published in the United States of America

Paperback ISBN: 978-1-62747-263-0

Ebook ISBN: 978-1-62747-262-3

Published in 2018

Cover design by Andy Brenits. Brenits Creative

Cover photo by Denys Bilytski

Contents

Dedication

To all of my seen and unseen mentors.
You are forever in my heart.

Preface

One of the definitions of *preface* that I found was "an introductory statement by the book's author setting forth its purpose and scope."

I pondered that definition and decided the purpose of this book is to experience and share said experience with those who might find my truth an awakening for them. The opportunity for me has been to peel back a few more layers of who I am and connect with energy that sees me through different eyes.

I'm anxious to have you take advantage of the view through my eyes and the eyes of the energies I found along my walk through the stars. The view for you ahead is an opportunity, on some level, to awaken, expand, or re-experience.

If you use your imagination and reach into the cosmos with your mental hands, don't be surprised if the universe reaches back and grasps your being while it whispers in your ear and speaks of your magnificence.

Section I

Wisdom begins in wonder.

Socrates

WRITING A BOOK IS NOT FOR SISSIES

I couldn't sleep. So I got up and took a 3 a.m. shower. I was still digesting my disappointment and lack of accomplishment going into the last day of a four-day, book-writing seminar in Sedona, Arizona. The seminar was meant to help me create my best-seller.

As I was drying off, I recalled a moment I'd had with my other half the first morning of the seminar. As everyone was settling in to start the day, I was getting all my writing tablets in place and noted how many tablets we'd brought with us. I said to her, "I don't know if I'm ready to write a book. I sure am glad I brought all these note pads, though, so I can do a lot of therapy on myself." She quipped, "I'm not sure you brought enough!"

It's funny that this exchange came up, because since we'd arrived for the seminar I'd been recalling many childhood happenings with the adults in my life. Including the worst possible emotional experience I can think of. Which, by the way, I hadn't thought of for years.

When I was in first grade, we lived in New Albany, Ohio, northeast of Columbus. It was a lot like Mayberry, USA. There was literally one small grocery at the main intersection of town and our farm was a couple of miles away from it.

At that time I had elected to play the saxophone. The school band was a big part of the world of New Albany and our band leader Mr. Grim was loved by all of us kids. Somewhere along the way, Mr. Grim had tangled with the powers that be at school and got himself relieved of duty. It was the beginning of a storm.

Somewhere in the middle of the upheaval with Mr. Grim, I observed my mother talking about the situation to someone else in town. My mother's overview of the situation with Mr. Grim was that she didn't see why everyone was so upset with his departure because the last time she had seen a program that he had put together, she felt it

3

really wasn't very good. What I was witness to was typical gossipy stuff, but my first-grade brain soaked it all in. The next sequence in the story is that somehow with my mother nearby but out of earshot, I ended up at the counter of the local grocery store. I'm not sure if I was asked or if I volunteered my mother's version of the bandleader's situation to the woman at the counter. Of course, I made it clear I was just passing on my mother's opinion and, of course, the woman at the counter knew my mother. I can recall the look on the clerk's face, as if to say, "Isn't that interesting." I was just gossiping like I'd heard adults do. I thought it was valuable information to pass on. My mother arrived at the counter to find me there ahead of her. Being none the wiser, she paid for her groceries and we headed home.

At some point after we arrived home, the phone rang and my mother answered it. I was playing and didn't pay any attention to the conversation. Soon after my mother came looking for me; I saw her walk in the room and she appeared to be half-way to 'boil.'

The next story segment that flashes through my mind regarding this incident is my mother questioning me about what I had said at the grocery store. I was a little puzzled because I knew she hadn't heard the exchange at the grocery store. How did she know?

What happened was the gossip train got a hold of my statements about my mother's opinions. Some unknown party considered the information offensive and forwarded it to someone else, which eventually took a path to my mother, who was caught with her foot in her mouth. I think this all happened before we had arrived home from the store!

I didn't know what hit me. It wasn't physical. My mother's voice started at about 20 decibels higher than normal. "How could you say such things about me? Don't you realize everyone in town will know what I said? You should be ashamed of yourself acting that way." She said she felt like a laughing-stock and never would be able to show her face again anywhere. All this energy was raining down on me from above as she continued her vocal attack.

I didn't know what to do. I was sure I had just annihilated my mother's life and I was the most horrible child on the planet. I was terrified and felt like the whole world was looking at me. There was nowhere to run and the fear-filled words and energy just kept coming. When I was finally able to get away from her, I felt I wouldn't be able to show MY face anywhere. I ran upstairs in our farmhouse to my bedroom over the kitchen crying my little heart out, not knowing what to do. I was so chagrined that I jumped over my bed and buried myself between the bed and wall next to it to try to make myself invisible. It wasn't working. I was still conscious and terribly shaken by what I'd done to my mother, feeling SO sorry. I didn't know how to fix it and I just lay there trembling. Hence my earlier comment about therapy!

As I was saying, I had really been looking forward to the Sedona writing event. The prospect of a possible career change was terribly exciting after being a plumber for more than 30 years. Imagine me, a born introvert, making it to the limelight as a world-renowned author. With great optimism I visualized giving my own seminars and having book signings with lines of people clamoring for my attention and words of wisdom. A security team would be holding the crowds back at all my future events.

I had come to the seminar certain that I'd produce an outrageously successful best-seller. The way all the pieces had fallen into place from the first exposure of the book idea, I was convinced that it was divine guidance to have ended up at this seminar. I figured I was in tow behind guardian angels that would put the right words in my head at the right time and I'd just put them down on paper. I was positive I could channel a book that would cause the earth to open up and spread inspiring messages to untold millions around the globe. To say the least, in my visions of my new future, my bags were packed.

Having been a full-time plumber and part-time spirit seer, I was wondering what a career as an author would be like. Prior to coming to the seminar, I thought the universe was going to magically pour this book into my brain. This was going to be my ticket to a new life. I thought it would be a simple process. The book within would be brought to the surface by the universe and then this best-seller was going to be a slam dunk. And I'd be off to the big time.

In my excitement, I had forgotten that things rarely go the way you think they will. After three days of creating, I saw no flow to my words. I wasn't receiving any content that I thought a writer of my visionary caliber should produce. I began to panic. For God's sake, I had no idea which way to go with the story. I figured with over six decades on the planet, I had reached guru status. This was supposed to be easy!

To distract my anguish for a moment, I had this silly little poem pop into my head. "So I'm sitting in a bedroom in Sedona, Arizona. It's as dark as it can be. I'm frustrated trying to write a book waiting for the powers that be. I wish the voices in my head would show up and tell me how to proceed."

I was raised in the era of strong, silent types. The Gary Coopers, the Steve McQueen, the John Waynes and the Clint Eastwoods. They were my models. One of the funny things about this is that over the years, I've been told on many occasions that I look like Clint.

These strong silent types emulated to me the way a man was supposed to act. You don't cry or show emotion. One wrinkle of an eyebrow and every order you gave was obeyed. And you always knew what to do. Plus, there was the added bonus of having women fall at your feet and look at you like mesmerized deer. That all appealed to me and I did my best to put out a little of that persona. I pulled off everything except the part about the mesmerized women at my feet and always knowing what to do.

I learned there's a penalty for being strong and silent, which is that no one knows who you are. You just walk around being cool and don't connect emotionally. There's no energy exchange so no one knows what's going on inside you. Those close to you suffer, as do you, because you miss out on the energetic connection.

When you are playing the strong-and-silent game, you also learn not to feel hurt or let anyone know when you have been hurt. You learn not to say anything about anything. You just hold things in until you finally explode and then you wreak havoc of untold proportions on those closest to you. That doesn't go very far in the game of wanting people to hang around you. Who would want to, after you let loose?

I learned at an early age that the way for me to get attention was to have a thing or gizmo or toy that no one else had. I never liked the status quo. I wanted my house and car to be different from everyone else's. It was part of the strong, silent thing. That way I didn't have to be loud or obnoxious; I could just stand there and look pretty with my new unusual thing-a-ma-bob and all eyes would be on me. If I could manage a way to own something unusual, then I was always willing to work for it.

For the most part, I got what I was after. When I was eight years old, I wanted a horse and every week I'd cut my grandfather's yard with his big riding lawn mower to earn money. I loved riding that thing. I was alone in my world and could control that beast of a contraption. I was in charge and the machine had to obey me.

Every week I got a dollar and then gave it to my dad and told him to save it for a horse. I learned how to look in the newspaper want ads and see what horses were for sale, and I'd call my dad at his office and tell him what I'd found in the horse column. I was consistent and persistent. That was my way of manifesting. I'd dream and visualize and dream some more and call my dad at work.

On my ninth birthday, she showed up. Sheri. She was a twenty-two-year-old Tennessee Walker. She came with a black, kid-sized, silver-studded saddle. OHHH, man! I got a lot for my money. Those one-dollar lawn jobs had added up fast.

Since I got the horse thing taken care of, what could I do next to be different and stand out in the crowd? Hmmmm. Why not check out seeing spirits? Yeah, that's a great idea. I'm going to look into mind-reading or fortune-telling or something weird.

So here I am on the morning of the last day of the Sedona writing seminar, scanning my mind for a way to salvage these four days and go home with something I consider a 'book.' I'm restless and anxious and awake very early in the morning. After three days of emotional ups-and-downs and cramped hands, I had managed to produce written content that I'd say was more of a personal therapy session than content for an admiring audience.

My tail is between my legs as I think about packing to go home after the final morning session. I've spent all this time and money for this event and I don't have a book. I'm going to have to be a plumber until I die! A thousand years from now, when my bones get excavated by an archeologist, the report of his or her findings will be that this skeleton was that of a common laboring peasant. I knew it; I'm a loser.

After my 3 a.m. shower, it seemed too early to get up and function so I quietly lay down on the bed in the dark hotel room. For no reason I started thinking about an insurance class I had in college that was taught by a man with an outgoing personality. He was just a nut about insurance; he loved all facets of it. He had been a Japanese prisoner of war in World War II and was forced to work in mines. Because of the health risk from that, he was deemed uninsurable as far as getting any kind of life insurance for himself.

His classroom was a lecture hall with fifty or sixty of us at each session. Not being there for any purpose other than it was a required course, I would drift off and go into my dream/visualization mode. I'd consciously tune in and out in the class and still try to appear interested.

I was sitting with a friend one day in a lounge area of one of the central buildings on campus, when my insurance teacher happened by and we struck up a conversation, just for conversation's sake. He commented on me being in his class. That was amazing to me because I had no idea he had noticed me. He said he felt I was never really there in his class. He meant that yes, I was there physically, but I wasn't there consciously.

Okay, I thought, I've been found out. I'm about to be told to get my act together. From his vantage point in the classroom, he could see I was off somewhere else in my head. The surprising thing was he thought that was a good thing.

Had I been a professor in the front of a room, I'd have taken that drifting off as being bored and not wanting to be there. He saw me as a dreamer and went on to say that dreamers, in his opinion, had it over non-dreamers. He felt that dreaming was a creative process that actually helped one get ahead. I don't remember acing his class but I felt a lot better about myself after what he said that day. It was a nice little gift from the universe to recall that story.

Maybe if I dream enough tonight I can come up with a story line. As my head hit the pillow I heard,

Are you ready to write this book?

I focused and clearly saw a man basically in my face. He looked like a normal person. His chin was resting on folded arms while he maintained an intent expression. I couldn't see his torso or what he was wearing. But there was no mistaking that he was there with the intent to contact me; I just wasn't expecting it. I didn't panic; he wasn't a physical person.

Having experienced spirit connect, I knew there was no reason to call hotel security because this encounter was showing up in my third eye. You know, that spot in your forehead between your eyes where you perceive and conjure images with your eyes closed.

That's where I meet a lot of non-physical visitors. This was a new and unexpected energy form for me. I didn't recognize him. But I could sure see him and feel the flow of the words in my mind.

Usually as I'm going to bed and just starting to go to sleep, I ask a question to the universe and see what I get back. I wasn't expecting someone to be in the doorway tonight, though.

I do like it when someone shows up. I don't have a lot of people hanging around me waiting to share my energy on a personal level. I move too fast, I think. And I'm not the life of the party, as it were. I'm too quiet and I watch and listen a lot. So when I get an astral traveler stopping by, I enjoy the connection. It's energetic and I feel like someone is interested in what I'm doing.

In light of my past three days, I mentally responded to the soundless voice addressing me. "Yes. Who might you be? I know you're not my grandfather," who had popped in two days prior. Then I felt compelled to mentally ask, "Are you a team leader, of sorts, on the project?" I was referring to my unwritten best-seller. I didn't expect him to say yes. I was just fishing.

Yes, I am. It would be more accurate of me to say that I represent a group of energetic beings that are here to help you learn who you are. You are not ready to write a book until you heal yourself.

My emotions fell into my stomach and my mind hit the mental brake pedal. I saw my best-seller fly out the window and then had a clear vision of a therapy group in a circle in the back room of a church. Okay everyone, just one minute here. Stop the trolley. What do you mean 'heal myself?'

Scott, you are in the middle of a big awakening, my friend. You do not understand the complexity of this process and the book is a giant part of it. Do not let this encounter spoil your intention to achieve.

Yes, you have indeed been introspective. However, you do not know who you are on the inside.

That statement generated a deep pause on my part. As I considered it, I got a full frontal picture of my visitor's dark robe that was open in the front with wide, white, vertical bands that ran up both sides of the open front and connected behind his neck.

Scott, your vision is clear and your intent is sincere, but you have not cleared the channels to your heart. Your heart isn't clear enough to proceed with the project. You are blocking your own creativity with your wounds from childhood that you do not consider wounds. The energies created by the hurts in life are stored in your body and need to be released. When you clutch at all of the generated and inherited wounds of your existence, you create energetic walls that block you from receiving universal radiance as well as allowing your own brilliant radiance to shine.

Scott, essentially it is our job to get you to the bottom of the hurt and help others do the same.

11

This is where I froze. I didn't have any idea what to do next. As I was digesting the connection that I just experienced, I said, "Could you tell me your name?"

GONAN

I had absolutely no reference point in my mind to relate to that name. So I asked, "How do you pronounce that?"

GOONAHN.

Okay, but that was messy to me. It wasn't easy to flip off the end of my tongue. Then I heard,

Just call me Gabe.

I found that to be a much better match for my high-speed, get-it-done persona. All of a sudden, everything in my universe got very quiet. "Gabe, are you still here?"

Yes, I am here.
Scott, the information you received over the last three days may seem scrambled to you at this moment. Please know that it is part of a process that is taking place. The seemingly convoluted words you have received do have a flow that will emerge. These previous days and words are not wasted, by any means. Your emotional experience of the

last three days was the precursor to this work. It had to be done. You are experiencing a bit of a crisis, we know.

Do not let it go to waste.

You had to be taken to a place of humble solitude as you are now. Your breakdown had to happen to prevent us from overshadowing your wounds.

Your wounds are deep and have been festering for years. There has been overcrowding in the storage tank where you put all the hurt and then went on your way. The storage tank is your heart. The pain you stashed there has not been flushed from your system, but simply put under the carpet. Your wounds were created by happenstance. Your coping mechanism was to bury things and push on. It is something only a strong-willed energy would do. It was all you knew how to do. We want to show you a different way.

You are at the edge of a healing process that you have been surrounded by but have not been aware of. So are many others. When you experience emotional pain and you react on any level, a message is sent to your being through your heart. The heart sends out the alarm and your persona chooses what to do with it.

I've never been aware of my heart having anything to do with my life other than moving blood. What you're expressing to me is new territory. I never equated my heart with any type of methodology of healing. Heartbreak is about as close as I could say I relate and that to me is simply emotional response. I don't see how healing has anything to do with my actual heart.

Oh, but it does. You would be surprised at the level of interaction between your heart and your mind. To discover what your heart can do and the part it plays is more than an adventure. It is a grand awakening.

Scott! Get going. You have this final day to create grandly!

What do I get going with?

Your stories and your awakening! To begin, tell some of the wounds of your childhood. The direction will be clear. You will get a sense of which ones to use. You could start with telling how you were hurt and where it happened.

Convey how you confided in no one and bore the responsibility all on your own little shoulders. Tell how, in your young mind, you took it on yourself to believe that you were wrong and the adults told you that you were responsible and you tried to make amends as a child by pleasing everyone in your family. You can describe how you felt from all the endless 'should-ing' that went on in your house. You were hurt, my friend, but you do not want to see it that way. Do not fear telling the truth about your experiences in life; be afraid of NOT sharing the truth. Your truth could be another's awakening. Tell the stories, for God's sake. It will heal you.

Gabe, there's just one concern for me in all of this and doing as you suggest. It seems to me that the world is full of books about recovery and the aftermath of going through ordeals to include journeys of mind and awakenings. Does the world need another book like that from someone like me?

I go through my day looking for answers like everyone else. I stumble here and there intellectually and I've never sat at the feet of theologians. I was hoping for something earth-shattering to pop in my head that would cut a swath of new understanding for me and for others. My stories aren't likely to be cutting-edge. I came to the planet; I grew up; I got aggravated with my parents; I made a lot of mistakes; I got married, had kids, and got divorced; I want to win the lottery. You know, all the usual stuff people do and all I know to do is just keep pushing on day to day. I don't know what any other way of living would be like. What stories could there be from my existence that haven't been heard before?

Scott, before you go and throw yourself over a cliff, take a deep breath and know that you are loved. That is a cliché to you, we understand, but none-the-less know that it is true. There is loving energy waiting to express its way through you in a way that only you can orchestrate. There are those who need to hear the messages and truths in your story, that they would not hear any other way. They will be drawn to you in a way that you can relate. You do not have to worry much about guidance from us. Your book is at hand and you know what to do. So proceed. The wounds of your childhood are deep, my friend. They have not healed. We cannot use you to tell our story until you tell yours. It is a painful journey at times and you have often looked deeply within. You have not hit the root of the process, however.

You have an audience of at least one. If nothing else, you can reread your own words and benefit from what you find yourself putting on paper. You need to know, however, that there is an audience in attendance waiting for the curtain to be lifted on the story that only Scott can deliver.

Do not become consumed with content or appearances. Just put on paper what you feel is genuine and appropriate. And more than anything else, please have fun doing it. Do not make creating this book a task full of drudgery with feelings of have-to. Do you understand? This book will have its own grand journey as does every book. No two books take exactly the same path.

Sometimes footprints intermingle, but all paths, even the ones that books take, are unique. Trust that your book will say what needs to be said and those who need to experience it will.

Okay, Gabe, I'll try to keep in mind to have fun no matter what. I don't know what that's supposed to look like. I'm going to trust that you'll nudge me in the direction I need to go because I'm complete in the feeling that I'm stumbling around here. I guess I'll begin with looking at all the childhood stuff that's been coming up over the last few days.

So here I was now, early on the last day of the writing weekend. I should have been done processing my world of inner wounds in, what, 15 minutes or so? If I had this right, I'm supposed to spill my guts. Not sure what I'm supposed to do, but then I never really do. Maybe I'll just start with some of the biggies I'm aware of.

It was still early so I decided to let my mind digest all that I had just perceived and get a little more sleep. When the alarm finally went off to start this final day at the seminar, I found myself in a quandary. For some reason, my mind went to Christmas.

As a kid I was totally intrigued with the concept of Christmas and that there could be this really big celebrity who could and would care enough to bring me what I wanted. All I had to do was follow the rules.

The concept was fostered well by the adults around me and there was always an answer to my questions of who, how, and why regarding the guy with the flying reindeer. I SO wanted to see this man surrounded in such mystery. I thought that would be cool. So I went with the flow and intrigue as long as I could. Then one day my enquiring mind had to know and my maturing intellect got the better of me.

When I was a youngster in Ohio, a lot of drug stores had small food counters off to one side of the store. I was out shopping with my mother and brother in a shopping center one day and we ended up at such a food counter. We ordered and sat in a booth, with my mother and younger brother sitting across from me. The food arrived at the table and I started to indulge in a gourmet, grilled-cheese sandwich.

At some point in the meal, it occurred to me that this would be a good time to ask. So with my brother being too small to understand what I was going to bring up, I popped the question. "Mom, is Santa Claus real?" I saw the look of concern on her face, which I didn't understand at the time. I think she was trying to choose her words carefully. I sort of had my mother on the spot. She knew there was no way out of this one. My question was too direct. I may not remember her exact words but she basically fessed up, "No, Santa is not real."

I guess you could call that life experience a defining moment. I had been so willing to engage in the concept of Santa that I was seriously crushed. I felt the tears start to well up in my eyes and I know my mother noticed, even though I was trying to hold them back. I didn't know if I was sad or mad. Had I been duped or spared?

As an adult I can tell you that finding out there wasn't a Santa Claus really pissed me off. Think about it. I had been told an untruth by people that I trusted and believed in. So what else are you putting out there that isn't really like you say it is? That type of interaction tended to create some trust issues for me.

In one fell swoop the house of cards had fallen with this new awareness. With Santa gone, it was only common sense that the Easter Bunny, the Sandman, and the Tooth Fairy went with him. There I was in outer space and no one could hear me scream.

So having side-tracked to that event in my life, I was back to the quandary with which I awoke. I continually look for things to believe in; do I believe in my new early-morning acquaintance or do I guard myself and wait and see how it goes? Will he turn out not to be real too? Interesting thought to have about a seemingly imaginary figure in my third eye. So for the moment, I'll stay in neutral. Everything he tells me will be true unless it isn't.

As I pondered, Gabe said to me,

That remembrance was a good place to start, Scott.

VIRTUAL COAUTHORS

On the first morning of the book-writing weekend there was an opening exercise where we were taught to tune into the right brain as part of the creative process. After that, we were led through another exercise to visualize the ethereal entities around us that were going to support us as we birthed our books.

As I closed my eyes and started the process, I clearly knew my grandfather was at the center of my perception. I could see that he was standing with a large leather-covered book in his arms that represented the finished product I would produce. There was also a gathering of many other entities standing in an arc behind him, like a choir with him as the lead singer front and center. I was taken aback by the number of entities I could perceive showing up to support this writing endeavor. None of whom I had any conscious recognition of. I was a little embarrassed. I hadn't thought of myself as having celebrity status.

It was also quite an emotional encounter for me because I was really attached to my grandfather. Being my dad's father, he and my grandmother lived in a house on the same farm property we lived on.

As a country kid I didn't call him 'Grandpa' or any of the other nick-names attached to grandparents. I called him by his first name. Howard. I used to enjoy being out with him because in public, my act of calling him by his first name always drew notice. In those days it was very unconventional to address an adult by their first name. I don't know how that came about but it was and still is very endearing to me. It was different and I knew it. It was a trademark of mine.

So my world took a big turn the day I heard that my grandfather had passed. It was January 1st of 1977. I had last seen Howard the previous October in Phoenix, having asked him to be in my wedding and he did me the honor of making the trip from Ohio. I noticed that he seemed to be in a very conscious and controlled state, as if he was taking everything in, yet he appeared okay. I remember thinking at the time he seemed a little off, energetically. The wedding went well and he and my grandmother returned to Ohio after the event.

As a kid I was practically attached to Howard's hip. He was essentially my father figure, go-to guy, and mentor. The inner, little me still misses him a lot. On some level I'm still looking for someone to ask if I'm doing things right. When I lost my grandfather, I lost all sense of 'which way do I go now?' I never replaced that special connection. Even as an adult I can bring myself to tears thinking about him.

I remember being in a window seat at night on the plane to Ohio for Howard's funeral service. I was in a daze. I felt closed in and lost as I stared out into nothingness. I was met at the airport by my father, who had arrived from California before me. There was the eventual gathering at the farm and seeing my grandmother. This wasn't normal

19

for me; I didn't know how to feel or what to say and think. I had never lost a major influence in my life before. The night before the funeral I remember sitting on a small landing to the upstairs of my grandparents' farm house, wondering how many times as a kid I had gone up and down those steps to find Howard or go to the bedroom down the hall where I'd sleep when I stayed overnight. What was I going to do without him as my anchor?

My grandmother was a tower-of-strength type and didn't seem to waver. If she ever broke down, I never witnessed it. By the time I arrived, she had already taken care of the funeral details and seemingly accepted this step in the circle of life.

The funeral was well attended. I sat in the back of the hall with no desire to remember my grandfather laid out in a casket. The usual memorials were uttered and I watched as my grandmother was the last to view before the lid was closed. So far I was holding it together and just wanted things to be over.

The next vivid recall of this trip for me was at his graveside. It was January and I was frozen to the core. The wind was blowing and there was a blanket of white on every inch of the cemetery. At the end of the last words, everyone started making their way back to the cars while I lingered alone. There was just me and a final moment in time with my grandfather as I had known him.

While standing alone there in the January wind, the finality of the situation finally hit me and I lost it. I was gasping for air and trying to keep from buckling physically. I didn't know what to think and I didn't like being out of control like this. I'd never had this happen and didn't know what out-of-control was supposed to look like. On the one hand, I was glad to feel something because I had been numb up to this point. On the other hand, I felt weak, vulnerable, and completely lost.

My only brother Kyle who'd come from California came back for me and basically escorted me to the cars. Somehow the world didn't stop turning. We all eventually returned to our routines and living went on.

Back in the seminar room, back in my vision center, I thanked the ethereal crowd for showing up and offering their support. My guess was we've all been together many times before in many places.

I mentally projected to the ethereal audience, "I'm so touched that you're all here." To quote an academy award moment, "You like me! You really, really, like me. My heartfelt thanks to you all and to Howard. I do so miss what we had."

Unexpectedly then I heard my grandfather.

Scott, I have to interrupt you here. I have to interject that you are a wonderful person and you do not have to idolize me on any level. I was touched by your delightful energy as a child. You were always excited and willing to participate. 'Inquisitive' was your middle name. You were the son I never had. I did not connect with your dad like I did with you. He was a different soul. You and I were much more in tune. I did not want to not be part of this book and I wanted to say before you moved on that as you feel grateful for our connection, know that I adored you and honor you for being of the heart you are. I, as a grandfather in this incarnation, felt you owed me nothing. I felt you were my mentor in many ways. The message for me to give you is do not be amiss in thinking that I served you; it is you who served me on any number of levels. Having said that, continue on your journey of greatness as you explore your heart.

When my grandfather finished, there was an additional message from energy behind him.

Your heart is calling to you to write this book. It has been a long time in the planning and orchestration. The moment is at hand for you to begin your new career. There is a timeline and you are on course. Do not let go.

Begin my new career? How did they know I was looking for another way of making a living?

We are here for you. You can do this book. It is a particular book that is timely and especially meaningful to your heart and many others. You will be touched by the energy of the universe as it invokes in you a stillness that you have never known. We have your best interests at heart and are willing to work with you at any time. You do not need to thank us. We need to thank you for volunteering for this. It is not often that someone such as you comes along and serves us as well as you have. It is much easier to stand back and let someone else step up. You stepped up and we thank you.

GROUP THOUGHT

During one of the seminar writing sessions, I heard, "This is not Gabe." Then the following manifested through my pen.

At this point in your receiving, we wanted to connect with you and those around you to share a concept that few consider. We understand it helps you to identify with a source but it is not necessary to know who we are. It is not necessary to praise us or call us by a title. We are here to connect with you on a mental basis; that is all you need to know. At times, there are individuals who may connect with you, but this morning we are a group energy that you are not aware of. You have not been in contact with us before.

We are called by your energy guidance to help promote the fact that you are surrounded with the forces of the universe and that you and others as well can connect and take advantage of this resource at any time. You have not begun to know who you are as individuals or as a race. As a race, you are developing faster scientifically than you are on a mental, intuitive level. That wording 'mental intuitive' might surprise you. All of you are able to intuitively connect. There is a symbiotic linkage by design for all of you on the planet that connects all minds. Some level of this understanding exists by those more cognitively in tune, but for the most part there are the masses that ramble through life unaware of the possible conscious connections that could be experienced.

Our part in the presentation of this information is fractional. We are simply a group energy drawn to share, explore, and elevate mankind when the opportunity presents itself. You can assign any name you feel is appropriate. We are dimensional travelers. We are familiar with the transition to group mental connection that your planet is trending toward. Until now it has not been popular conversation at the coffee shop to sit around and discuss how individuals can best bridge their minds. If you knew the benefits of group-connect you would be anxious to participate. You have all experienced group thought in life.

As an example it is the utterance of the same word at the same time by two people. Imagine hundreds of people having the same utterance.

The process of group-connect on this planet is not unknown. Centuries before now your race knew the process of group-thought. You have been led by events and happenings into a cycle that took you all away from the group-thought process.

Many beings of the time were staggered by the loss when the connection ended. The disconnect could be likened to suddenly finding yourself on a distant planet alone and unable to call home. Those who were left, who could still connect, dwindled in numbers and the art form was lost.

You as a group today do not realize how alone you are because it is all you know. There is no invasion in group-connect. You still maintain your individuality while being connected on an energetic level. You experience a sensation akin to that of holding hands with another at your side while walking down the street. Only you are holding mental hands with millions. When the last great disconnect occurred, there was chaos, of sorts.

Just imagine being in an order of existence and having a way of living you are familiar with suddenly taken away from you. It was confusing and disconcerting.

In time, life resets as it does and living goes on. Legends emerge to carry the stories until they lose their way to time and forgetfulness. Then the lore is no more and no one knows what was.

That is your current state on this planet. The mass of the population is unaware of the processes of the past. It was long ago and the cycle is beginning to come around again. There will be a time in the future when your planet will experience group thought that will have its beginnings in your now.

We do not wish to represent ourselves as extra-terrestrials or beings from another dimension that are going to come through a portal and take over your planet. The intent of this communication is to give you a sense of what was and what is to come. We are planting ideas as seeds. It is not important to know who we are or where we reside. We see the need to prepare those who are open to the topic and wish to expand their minds to possibilities.

Some of you will scoff at the idea of group-thought and others will embrace the concept to the point that it could be attempted. If nothing else in your realm, just having the concept in your mind will open other doors of thought and reflection that will give you new opportunities of experience. Let us say it is almost like having another tool in your tool box. You may not need it today but you might need it tomorrow.

I can sense you're waiting for me to see you, Gabe.

What did you think of that?

I don't know. I certainly found it compelling, for sure.

Scott, you do not need to be consumed and feel that you have to take steps in a certain direction. I just wanted you to experience energy other than my own that might influence thought on your part or the part of others.

Thanks, Gabe. I enjoyed that.

LEARN WHO YOU ARE

Hi, Gabe. You must want me to push on. I can mentally see that you're pressing my hand to the paper to begin.

Gabe, I'm not sure why but I'm going with my instincts here. The story that's coming to me doesn't logically seem like it's presented at the right time but I feel obliged to share it.

That is quite a normal reaction to have. Just go with what feels right.

I was flying a rented plane one day over the desert northeast of where I live in Arizona. I lined the plane up on a wash to practice making an emergency landing. As I got near the point of ending the practice landing, I noticed some high ground to my left where the plane was close to the terrain, while the desert to my right was open. Being that close to land on one side gave me a sensation of speed that you don't get when you're up at higher altitudes. It was exhilarating to see the desert flash by!

I flew this way until the high ground dropped off and the stream bed turned away to my left. Then I pushed the throttle in and climbed back up to the right to do it all over again; I wanted to buzz the terrain one more time.

When I got the plane high enough to start the second practice emergency landing, I lined up over the same wash with the high ground on my left. But then I had an uncomfortable feeling and a thought that maybe I shouldn't do this. I'd had my fun on the first run and maybe I should just go on. So rather than descend I stayed up where I was and I could see one more time where high ground dropped off and the stream bed turned away under me. I visually followed it to my left as it flowed away from the plane. To my surprise, there was a low-flying helicopter coming up the wash in my direction. Had I made another low pass over it, the high ground wouldn't have allowed me to see the helicopter coming my way!

When I saw the helicopter below me I got scared about what could have happened. My low-altitude run would have put me in the helicopter's proximity where the high ground dropped off and met the wash. I wouldn't have seen the helicopter coming and he and I would have been at the same place at the same time. That's not a healthy thing to experience when flying. My heart was beating a little faster just thinking again about what could have happened.

Scott, the importance of this story is that the incident did not happen. The reason it did not is because you were in tune with who you are. Do you see where I am going with this?

You are in tune unless you are not. That happens to all people. Those that are in tune experience a smoother ride than those that disregard the signals. There are paths to walk and there are paths that should be avoided. Simply tuning in and being aware of your processes of mind alters a lot of wrong turns in the life experience. That is not to say that you will not have an experience if you take a misguided turn. Either way you WILL have an experience; however, some experiences can be more fatal than others. The object is to experience on as many levels as you desire without slipping off the razor's edge.

I would like to plant a seed of thought about your helicopter experience. If you had found yourself colliding with a helicopter, think about which outlook you would have chosen to participate in. Would you have chosen to experience, "Wow, this is interesting I am crashing into a helicopter. Let me make sure I fully experience this." Or would you have gone into fear and panic and missed out on the sensations of the crash? Maybe as a better example, imagine you are just flying along in your plane and one of the wings falls off. Would you enjoy the fall and have the experience of what the fall might feel like? Or would you generate fear, panic, and discord? The seed I am trying to plant here is no matter what experience you are participating in, it is in your best interest to fully enjoy it. So if you find yourself colliding with a helicopter, then be certain to have fun while you are doing it.

Consider this, Scott. Know that to say, "Wake me up when it is all over," is a valueless process. If you are not awake while everything is going on, essentially you are uncreating yourself. So as you see yourself about to collide, be aware of who and where you are and embrace the experience.

Now you have me wondering if I want to fly anymore. I hadn't thought about having fun during the fall to the ground after one of my wings falls off! I hope I can remember to enjoy all of that if it should happen. I can see where that would be a completely different way of looking at any event. It would also take a lot of the fear out of the happening, would it not? Or at least maybe one could experience fear instead of stark terror. I imagine it would take a lot of practice to elevate my thinking to a non-reactive state and simply experience whatever is in front of me.

Scott, that is the objective of the soul. The soul wants to transcend the fear level and simply experience. The soul wants to see, taste, feel, and hear the wind. It wants to know what it is like to race a meteor in space. It wants to know what it is like to stand on the highest mountain and try to see where the sky ends. The soul is thirsty for experiential sensation and wants to find out what it is like to touch another's heart. It can only do that in human form and you, my friend, volunteered to be the vehicle for your soul to safely do such things. You embraced the soul and said, "I will be the capsule that houses and protects you as you explore the wonders that await."

Scott, you and all humankind are a grand sort that stepped up and said, "I will let you learn and experience through me. I will help you learn and will gladly support you in your desire to experience all that is. I am you and you are me."

So when the occasion arises that you wonder what you are doing here, the answer, simply put, is that you are experiencing. You are holding the ticket and getting on the next amusement ride to see what thrill it can afford you. Then you get on the next and the next. It is a very simple process. Yet humans want to attach so many meanings to the process that it gets lost. Just experience and live and love and fight if you feel you need to experience that. But fight with no fear! Experience with enthusiasm and know that when your blind exuberance gets you in over your head, there is a helping hand behind you to cushion the fall.

Gabe, that all sounds so wonderfully simple and easy to apply but the picture you're painting seems like a fairy tale. There are days that I don't want go through. There are experiences that I don't enjoy and I get called into situations that I don't give one hang about. Where does all of that fit into this simplistic picture you're painting? It's as if you're saying everything is supposed to be fun with blind abandon. I'm not experiencing a life like that. I'm not complaining, just trying to fit what you're describing into the reality I perceive and I'm not coming up with a match.

Scott, the simple truth is you have not learned how to enjoy life with blind abandon. Can you accept that?

Yes I can own that. I know I have a lot of evolving to do.

If you can accept that then you are half-way to understanding the answer to your own question. We are describing a reality of perfect design and that design is possible to have. We are painting a picture of reality that you can experience if you are geared to achieving it. It is out there if you want to find it. Many get lost along the way because the vision gets blurred by seemingly every-day, mundane activities. The lives that many experience are counter-intuitive and happen without conscious thought for the outcome.

If you simply run out into oncoming traffic without conscious thought of which way or how fast the cars are moving, chances are you might find yourself in an unpleasant situation. The same thing applies in daily life experience. Give conscious thought to your next move and avoid the next pitfall to the extent that you can. Do not just run on automatic pilot. It is like steering a boat on a river at night with nothing but moonlight to see by. You know who you are. You know what you are doing. But the river ahead is a little dark and you have to keep a vigilant eye on the course ahead. If you do not, you could run aground.

So you're saying that I need to be conscious of every move and thought. It sounds like you mean every breath needs to be calculated. My perception of what you're saying is that to have an enjoyable life of blind abandonment, I can never relax. Are you saying I have to think about every move? If it's that much work, it's no wonder most of us don't achieve that level of living.

Scott, you are making this more difficult than it needs to be. Simply enjoy life as you encounter it on a daily basis. Do not project yourself into the future or dwell in the past as you go through your day. Notice the flowers in the pot on the way to a customer's front door. Notice the picture on the office wall when you walk by. Watch the body language of two people talking. Observe the bird sitting in the tree outside the window. Maintain curiosity about every breath you take and be aware of the flow of the air in and out of your lungs. This is living with blind abandon, in a sense. You are getting your money's worth when you tune into life. This can all be done as you go about your day, doing what needs to be done to live the physical life.

If you tune into what is going on around you, all the other fears and complications you tend to dwell on go away. Does this make sense? I am saying to function as you need to go through your day, but be aware and observant and amused by all that is going on around you. Enjoy the witness process. Learn a different way of being from noticing another's movements. Be appreciative of the opportunity to marvel at the sheer magnitude of all the happenings of physical life. I am simply saying take time to stop and smell the roses. That is why you chose life.

I like what you're suggesting. However it seems a little overwhelming to me at this point and somewhat of an impossible task. What would I do first to develop that type of thinking or way of being? Can I do it in this life or do I have to keep coming back until I get it?

It begins now with the desire to achieve the results. Keeping focus in the back of your mind is the tool. Focus is the bodyguard that stands behind you and does not let anything get in your way. Focus is the giant energy that looks over your shoulder from behind for all that is in front of you to see. Your focus uses its presence to deter anything in front of you that wants to block you from your goal. So begin today with the intention of achieving no fear. Maybe you can be done by tomorrow. Maybe you can be done in, say, five or six lifetimes from now. It does not matter. What else do you have to do? No matter how long it takes, be on the path and enjoy the process. What matters is to have the goal in mind and your focus standing behind you.

To answer your direct question of what you would first do, the first thing you do is DECIDE TO DO IT.

Gabe, thank you for being patient with me. I want to get this right. I know that I keep asking the same questions. I just don't want to miss the mark.

Scott, you are not missing anything. Quite the contrary. You strive for excellence in all you do and you want to touch the hand of God. You already have, on many occasions. You and others just do not realize it. So keep doing what you are doing and enjoy the adventure and please have fun with it. We look over your shoulder to help you focus and clearly wave one finger of caution to anything that attempts to block you. We love you and want to see you achieve whatever it is that attracts your interest. For now stay in tune and stay in the moment and simply enjoy being in the physical.

Gabe, it sounds like you're saying if that's all there is, then let's just keep dancing because nothing else matters.

In a sense you are correct, Scott. But be aware that while you are dancing, you still have some housekeeping chores to do. You still will have the mundane to deal with. It is just part of physical life. Your soul knew that coming in. We are saying just focus on what you are doing at any given moment and try to make a game of it. It does not have to be hard. In fact, the ease with which you can go about your day will astound you, once you find the sweet spot of focus on the moment.

When you fly an airplane, for the most part you are totally consumed with the experience of the plane functioning and your part of the equation, keeping the plane operating correctly. You are focused on the experience. You are one with the flying experience the entire time you are in the plane. That is why you like to fly. You are living in the moment and nothing else matters. The goal is to take that process into your day-to-day experience. Live your day like you are flying an airplane with constant focus.

Does that help you?

Yes, Gabe. I like that example. I know that others might experience the living-in-the-moment thing with other venues like painting a picture or making a quilt and so on. I realize that for me, flying a plane is the ultimate way to be in the now. I'm in the moment the entire time I'm flying a plane. I usually don't want to come back down. I see what you're saying. Basically, be totally into the experience of whatever I'm doing.

You are starting to see through different eyes, Scott. Just keep that focus and the process will evolve and elevate you.

THE POPPY

As I get quiet and do more pondering of the past, what pops up is a memory of the orange poppy. I'm somewhat resistant to putting this story together. And I find the realization of that awareness interesting.

When I was very young, if you stood at our kitchen sink and looked out the window, you could see the garden that was about 50 feet away on the other side of our gravel drive way. The view of the garden on this particular day included an older cherry tree suitable for climbing. Which as a young boy I did.

There was a single, orange poppy growing near the base of the cherry tree. I had offered to pick it for my mother previously but was told not to. "Just leave it there," she said. On this day, though, I cast all such instruction aside.

I really liked flowers as a kid and I still do. My neighboring grandmother had a huge daffodil patch that I'd salivate over but wasn't allowed to go near without supervision. On occasion I'd be allowed to pick some of the daffodils. That was close to kid nirvana for me. There was something about holding a bunch of flowers in my hand and smelling them that tripped my endorphins. Maybe I have an unrecognized flower fetish.

This day I could no longer restrain myself. I just wanted to pick that flower and give it to my mother. My small child persona was on a mission. Mom was going to be so surprised. So I did it. I picked the orange poppy with enthusiasm and ran into the house with my floral trophy in tow. I fully expected to be rewarded, praised, and adulated like a conquering hero. "Mom, look! I picked the flower for you." The statement, "I told you not to do that," came along with a scornful look on my mother's face. Needless to say my heart sank because the experience of presenting my mother a flower with child-like exuberance didn't really turn out the way I had expected.

Looking back I think she could have handled my presentation in a better way. Like, "Oh, honey, that's so pretty but next time let it stay in the garden where it can grow. Let's put it in some water for now."

I was discouraged, to say the least, and saddened to have disappointed my mother. I had expected her to be elated. The fall-out for my little heart was tremendous. I felt like I'd been cast from favor and really messed up – I was WRONG.

I don't really have a moral to the story except to say I'm sure it shaped me in some way.

There is nothing to add to the story. Your mother was not in touch with her sensitive side in that moment. But as an example to those reading this, it is important to see how damaging an adult response can be if one does not take into consideration what is seen through the eyes of a child.

THE TRAP

My mental shutter is clicking again, recalling a family vacation in northern Ohio. It was at a resort on Lake Erie where we had our very own cabin. The lake was only a few hundred yards from the front of the cabin and there was a beach area between our door and the water.

I'm feeling chagrined even as I start to recall this memory. I'm not sure what my inspiration was, but on this morning I had the bright idea to dig a small pit in the sand near some shrubs that were growing in a narrow section of the beach area. I dug it as deep as my childhood arm could reach and then I covered the hole with small sticks, paper and sand. The effect was essentially a small, invisible, animal trap. Or an invisible human trap, depending on what living thing happened to weigh more than the sticks and paper could support.

My snare looked like sand and was perfectly camouflaged so anything walking aimlessly down the beach might stumble into it and be captured. My juvenile mind reveled at the ingenuity.

My discomfort is building even as I get further into this story. And as I now think back, it seems like a horrible thing to have done, although at the time it seemed like a fun thing to do. The only rationale I can come up with is that, being somewhere between the age of five and seven, I must have had a frontal lobe that wasn't fully developed. Somehow the making of the trap appealed to my creative side.

Of course, as I was looking at the finished product, I was thinking what good was building a marvel such as this without something to actually spring it. I looked down the beach. "Hey, Mom!"

The rest is predictable. I guided my mother on a path that was sure to snare her right leg. I was right. My creation worked flawlessly.

I don't know what this action on my part said about me but my mother had a lot to say about the event. I recall something like, "I could have broken my leg!" (I hadn't thought about that!), as being part of her selection of emotional responses. Looking back I can't believe I did what I did and, as I mentioned before, I still feel chagrined about even relating the story. Maybe I was getting even for the orange poppy event. If it's healing to tell this story, so be it. I'm not feeling so triumphant.

The event said a lot about you, son. It said you did not have a lot of respect for your mother on a level of consciousness surrounding your relationship with her. Her relationship with you was one of possession, envy and control. She was a strong-handed disciplinarian, based on her experience as a child around her father. He ruled with an iron fist and she, being the oldest, knew no other form of example other than what she had as a model. She did tone her treatment of you down from what she had experienced as a child. You were the lucky recipient of a watered-down version of her father, the grandfather you never knew. This included her treatment of your father. He received far less scorn from your mother than your grandfather did from your grandmother.

The importance of the example here is that you contrived a trap to snare your mother because you felt trapped as a child. And you felt unsafe because of the strong treatment. You could not free yourself and you chose to express some tyrannical energy against your mother. You would not have done that to your father or neighboring grandparents, for several reasons. You looked up to your father more and you respected your mother less than you think. She represented malice to you. She represented 'shape up or ship out' to you. That is how she was treated and she did not know any other way to be. Do you see?

Yes. I'm feeling a little sad about all of that as I think back on it.

Scott. Let the sadness come up. That is the healing part for you. Now you can be more at peace with the event and if nothing else, your heart is cleansed a little more and there is a little less of a wall around it, which lets you more easily radiate to the world who you really are.

So, Gabe, simply recalling an event is healing? It doesn't always feel good to recall such things. At least not to me, anyway.

Scott, healing is a process. First being willing to recall things takes courage. That is the door opener. Next comes the willingness to forge ahead with the recall, knowing that you might feel uncomfortable. That is an act of bravery. Then to vocalize the recall is icing on the cake.

The fear you might have about the process is because it is not something you do on a regular basis, or you might not ever have done it at all. The trick is to do it the first time.

Gabe, your having said that brought to mind the first time I dove head-first off a high diving board. I stood at the top of the board looking at the water below wanting to do the dive, but I was afraid of what it might feel like because I had never done it before. After having a mental conversation with myself, I thought, "What the heck," and just did it. It was exhilarating and gratifying at the same time. Actually it was a little cleansing in a sense. By pushing myself into the action of diving head-first, it released all the apprehension I had about the actual feat. I felt lighter emotionally after I just did it.

That is an excellent analogy. The healing process can be exhilarating and cleansing and gratifying, as well. The painful part is actually the dread that you might create from the fear of actually doing the process. You went through that on the diving board. You spent more time being afraid of the dive than you did finally doing the dive. You learned a lot on that occasion. Pat yourself on the back for facing your fear and doing it anyway. You found out it was easier and less consuming to face the fear and interact, than it was to fearfully anticipate actually engaging in the action.

Just an aside on our part – it is interesting, do you not think, that you picked an analogy that literally involved diving into a situation head-first.

I hadn't thought of that. Well, look at me! I'm amazing!

Yes, you are! Truly.

Section II

You have your way. I have my way.
As for the right way, the correct way, and the
only way, it does not exist.

Friedrich Nietzsche

DON'T BE ASHAMED OF WHO YOU ARE; SEE IT, FEEL IT, BELIEVE IT

Scott, let me be in the spotlight here for a moment.

There is a message that is strong and clear that has been advocated in many ways for many ears and hearts to receive. The message is so clear that often the intended recipients miss the true message. Here it is – BE WHO YOU ARE AND NO ONE ELSE.

It is up to you to be who you are and plan your own agenda. There is no higher message that can be delivered. There are those of you who will present arguments against such a statement but understand that such arguments take second row to this message.

Those among you who reject the notion of understanding self-first are entitled to your perspective. There is a concept being presented here that will elevate those who are ready to understand. Then there are those of you who will resist the saying. It is okay either way. There is a gift here for those who want to take advantage of it.

Those of you who feel that truth has not been spoken are invited to try the concept on for size. The proof is in the pudding. One should try new tastes; the palate will guide you as to pleasure or displeasure. This thinking will fit for some. Others will not be willing to try at all. And some will try half-heartedly and feel no connection. At least, for now.

Who you are as a person of source may differ from those around you. Exploring new concepts is much like trying a new recipe in a cook book. Some explore the recipes in the cook book more diligently than others. Two cooks in the same kitchen could conceivably produce a different-tasting dish using the same recipe. This could happen by virtue of the attention given to exact measurements or to details and quality of ingredients being used. Interestingly enough when the finished dishes are placed side-by-side, the more palatable dish will emerge by simply tasting the end result.

Those doing the tasting will be better suited to make the decision as to which dish is better than those who simply view the prepared food before them. The beauty of the taste test is that no one is wrong. All who taste the cuisine and make decisions based on their taste buds will share one marvelous thing. They will all get to experience the dish and decide if they want to have it on an ongoing basis.

Scott, let us look at you as an example. You are finding your rhythm with the ability to connect with this side. You have always been connected. You were not fully aware of your connection until lately. However, you have unwittingly used the process to facilitate your access to your surroundings and those around you.

You fail to see the true benefit of the gift.

Scott, I see that the word 'gift' bothers you, does it not?

Yes, I feel uncomfortable.

You should not. It is who you are. You feel that you have worked to get it and you feel that your abilities are substandard compared to mentors of past.

Yes, I would say that is somewhat true.

So Scott, would it be safe to say that in a sense you are ashamed of who you are?

No, Gabe, I wouldn't say 'ashamed' so much as 'frustrated.'

Scott, you have to temper your thoughts about yourself. You are quite advanced in your thinking and outlook toward other souls. You have been in the game a long time. You do not give yourself credit for your talents. You will soon open up even more toward your vision of knowing and intuitive ability. There are many who know how to see. You are one of them. You have a strong suit. You need to know that your abilities are not tempered by concern for what is said. You relay honestly and do not hold back and you should feel honored that those who will come to you will come for that honesty.

Being who you are is not and has not been an easy task. You have stood your ground more than once. Even when it was frightening, you never faltered. We are proud of you. You did not back down. Your fortitude was stellar and you always knew how to play the game when it counted. Does this resonate for you?

Yes, Gabe, it does and yes, I've tried to learn to not be afraid. I'm confused though about why you'd go out of your way to express this to me now. I'm honored by your vision of me. But this isn't something that would go in the book. So I'm surprised by the side-bar, as it were.

Scott, we see you in a different light than you see yourself. We are being complimentary to give you a chance to accept a view of yourself that you do not embrace.

You compare yourself to others who seemingly have achieved more than you have. Be very clear in the process

45

of knowing who you are, that you excel and stand out in the crowd among those that dare to dance with the spirit of the moon.

Gabe, I don't understand what you mean by 'spirit of the moon.'

We mean that you attract the notice of a lot of energetic beings. You do not realize how many unseen mentors are at your side tending your path of expansion. The promising student always draws the attention of the professor. Those who thirst for the experience are led to the front of the line. You know what we mean. We simply applaud your tenacity and true caring of the gift of building souls.

Part of your being on the planet is to lead others to awareness and build them to be kings, and you are doing so in the early stages of this new adventure.

There's that discomfort thing again on my part, Gabe. For you to tell me that I was put on the planet sounds like I'm some messiah. I don't have any sense that that's who I am. I don't think I'm ready to claim that title. I'm just Joe Average. I work six days a week. I put in long days and I worry about paying the mortgage just like everyone else does. And oh, by the way, my parents weren't exactly Joseph and Mary, in any sense.

Scott, it is not a matter of claiming a title. It is learning to be comfortable with who, in fact, you are. And who you are is unique. Including your malfunctions. There is no one such as you. There is no one on the planet who has your vision of reality. And there is no one on the planet such as your neighbor. You are unique and so is your neighbor. You claim no title other than 'Scott.' You are humble and gentle to those who seek you out. You hold no attachment to another's evolution. You use a guiding hand to encourage them ahead on the path, if they are willing. You have not taken advantage of another. Your tendency is to over-compensate in others' favor. You let others learn, yet you are willing to give guidance to point out possible pitfalls.

Gabe, if I'm that unique, or let's use the word 'fabulous,' why am I not more content with who I am? I never feel like I'm doing anything right, in a sense. I feel like I'm stumbling through life on a daily basis. When will I be okay with my existence?

The answer to that, Scott, is you will be okay with it when you are okay with it.

Let us say that you have a passion for making chocolate cakes. And for whatever reason others around you have a chance to experience your chocolate cakes. Then suppose that those who have tasted your wares have occasion to tell you that you make a mean chocolate cake. You have some choices now as to how you can experience those words expressed to you. You can choose to accept the compliment, say "Thank you," and feel gratified. Or you can hear the adulation and emotionally react and let the voices in your head negate the experience of the compliment. Do you see?

47

I think so, Gabe. If I have this right, you're saying that once again I choose the experience to have and that I can embrace or shun the energy being sent in my direction.

You encapsulated that very well. So accept our adulation of the moment and be at peace. There is no more to share on this note here. But we would like to add that it is our genuine position that you should consider putting this previous exchange in the book. It is who you are and you benefit from not being ashamed of it.

Thanks for your guidance on all of this, Gabe. Truly, I do appreciate it.

THE BOTTLE

I'm scanning back through my memory banks and recalling a black-and-white photo of me about six months old. I'm propped up on a pillow on my parents' bed with a beer bottle on the pillow next to me. My mother is nicely dressed and sitting on the edge of the bed to my left.

Now I'm trying to see this picture in a new light. The beer bottle was probably intended as a joke and I've always taken it that way on the occasions I've seen this print. But I was always struck by the fact that I wasn't being held by my mother in that picture. In fact, I don't have any pictures of my mother holding me. To some, that might imply lack of connection. Hmmmm. I don't know where to go beyond that consideration.

You might consider the fact that heartfelt connection was not present in this relationship, though your mother cared for you physically. She was too consumed with her own issues to connect with you on an emotional level. She did not know how to do that. You were the recipient of half a mother. Not to say she was evil on any level, just unnatural herself and passing it on to you. Like you she had a mother who did not have strong nurturing skills.

For having had the parental experience she had, your mother did a decent job of breaking the pattern. She was highly insecure as a result of that. Hence she was self-consumed or perhaps untrained as an emotionally-connected mother. Try to see the good in your mother to the extent that she was doing the best she knew how to do. Keep in mind that there is not a statute of limitations on behavior patterns, unfortunately. There is no buzzer or alarm that warns one when they are not being an evolved person. People learn when they learn.

That's where I lose my patience at times. I tend to want it all right now and I want others to get it now also. I forget that others aren't on my timeline and that they have their own process in place.

That is a growth point for everyone to be aware of. One needs to allow developmental space for others to operate in. All souls are not on the same time schedule. So be patient with yourself and others in the expansion process.

Okay so just tap me on my shoulder when you see me forgetting, please.

Deal!

LIONS AND TIGERS AND BEARS, OH MY!

I was playing outside one summer day with other kids behind the house of a friend of my mother. We had gone over there for what would now be called a play date. There were some kids there that I didn't know and I remember not really being part of the crowd. For the most part the other kids were older than I was.

The mothers were inside the house as we ran around and screamed outside. We were all little, I know, because at some point a game we were playing caused us to end up under a wooden picnic table in the back yard. The game turned into scary storytelling. One story line in particular turned into, "We're all safe under the picnic table and should stay here so the lions that are in the neighboring trees and bushes won't eat us." That one got my attention! For some reason I bought into the story and started to become very frightened. I didn't want to let the other kids know how scared I was, so I played it cool as I sat panicking in my corner of the safe zone under the picnic table fortress.

I was really taking this lion thing to heart. I couldn't understand at the time why the other kids were seemingly taking this information in stride. I was ready to bolt but I didn't get that energy from any of the other kids. My internal reaction was something like, "My God, you guys, there are lions out there – we can't just sit here." I saw no forces being mounted to deal with the lions so I figured it was time to take things into my own hands. I did what any small child with a survival instinct would do. I bolted. It was every man for himself. I hit the back door of the house looking for my mom.

The mothers were engaged in a front room and I didn't know whether to barge in or hang around the edge, knowing my mother wouldn't appreciate being bothered. I figured that in the immediate moment the lions couldn't get into the house so I went for the hang-around-the-edge tactic. Finally I was noticed and granted permission to approach. I quietly laid out my concerns to my mother about the pending doom outside which to me was VERY real – all I wanted was to be scooped up and protected. And I fully expected that to happen. But it didn't! I was basically told there were no lions, "So go play." "But mom, there are lions, the other kids said!" She sent me the same energy again and the conversation among the mothers continued. What I did next isn't really clear in my memory, but the falling ax for me was not being recognized as needing to be protected.

It was really one of those big moments that make up who you are for the rest of your life, I think. Because of that moment I never shooed my kids away for anything when they would come running up to me. I wanted them to know I was there for them in case they had lions chasing them in the back yard.

I always wanted them to feel safe because I knew how not-fun it was to be scared. I wanted them to know that they could come to me any time they needed to be scooped up. I also wanted to cover my bases with my kids and break the chain of what was handed down in my lineage and perhaps show them a different way.

Scott. Do you want some input?

Sure, Gabe. I enjoy hearing your take. I was just processing what I recalled. I felt the emotion come up again as I relived the experience in

51

a way that I have never felt it before when I would remember that incident. I normally would just feel resentment recalling that day.

You are healing, my son. This is the process. Remember, relive, and then let the energy slide past you as you assimilate the experience. Your being wants to be heard and recognized like the little boy under the picnic table. It wants to be recognized and protected. Do you see how this works now? You have never dissected these events in your life. You have relived them many times in your mind but you never let the lions out of the cage, as it were. You kept them inside as a child and then also as a teen and as you got older you kept them buried inside, pushing them aside thinking they were no longer relevant. They are always relevant until you disconnect the chains.

The chains are energetic, of course, but they may as well be made of steel because they hold you back on a lot of levels. They shield your heart energy and block your radiance. They have the same effect as a drug that makes you groggy and slows your reflexes. As you clear these events and the emotions around them, you clear channels of communication between you and the universe.

The universe is waiting to pour into your heart and being. It is blocked by the energy you carry stored in the memory banks. It wants the shelf space that is being used by the childhood hurts. Do you see? So when you do this recall and energy releases, it clears the way for higher communication. The higher communication wants to reach into your soul and connect. It is that supportive. It wants to scoop you up and protect you. It will not let the lions eat you.

Thank you, Gabe. I've never had it put to me that way. And I just realized something. I've gone through life afraid that the lions were going to eat me, in a sense.

Now you know that the lions are not real but you have lived still waiting for them to jump out of the bushes. Do not fear my son; we will help keep the lions at bay. The only lions out there are the ones you create.

Gabe, I guess I know that. But I forget to keep that thought in the front of my brain.

The lions are, for the most part, self-generated from within. You are so busy generating lions that do not exist that you block the universe on yet another level. Do you see, my child, how this works?

I never looked at it that way. I don't think of myself as blocking. Maybe I am. I do think of myself as protecting my being. I know I'm good at putting up barriers.

Please note that you used the word 'barriers.' You do not realize how significant it is for you to bring that word into the conversation.

I'm not sure what you mean, Gabe. I was just contemplating how I put up emotional barriers to protect myself from perceived non-physical attack. I'm pretty sure every other person on the planet does the same thing.

Yes, for the most part, that is true. We are leading up to something here. What you do not realize is that emotional barriers are not the only walls that humans put up to protect themselves. The greatest wall that a person creates for protection is the heart wall.

Gabe, you took me by surprise with the term 'heart wall.' I've never heard of that before.

Heart wall refers to the energetic blockade that one can build around the heart. You can figuratively create etheric structures that encircle a physical heart much like the rings of Saturn.

If you could see what we can see, you would be witness to energy that radiates from your heart center. It can look like circular military bunkers. You might even see steel or concrete-type energy warding off the robust attacks of life.

Every time your persona experiences an emotional upheaval, your brain and your heart work together to generate energetic blockades to prevent future emotional hurt. Over the course of a lifetime, one can end up with protective energy that can project a distance many feet from the physical body. The barriers are subtlety constructed and become the norm and one does not realize how much energetic armor they are carrying around. You have created some pretty heavy barriers around your heart, my friend. This protection, as you might call it, only hinders you. Especially regarding the universal connection that you long to establish and maintain.

Your heart is so busy dealing with the interference of the protective layers around it that it cannot do the job it was meant to do. That job is to radiate universal awareness.

The heart is continually trying to maintain connection with mind, matter, and the universe. With all the armor in place, what the heart goes through trying to connect is like one person trying to talk to another under water.

Visualize an exuberant child full of fun, expression, and playful energy that gets excited about anything it encounters. Next mentally see this same child encumbered with big elastic bands that limit their movement. This child can still move physically, but each movement takes extra exertion because the bands are so restricting.

You, my friend, are experiencing the same type of restriction. You are so familiar with it that you accept it as the norm. If you were to instantly drop the energetic barriers you have erected around your physical heart, you would experience a lightness of body and mind that you have forgotten existed. Then you would crave solitude, quiet, and rest while your heart processes this new unencumbered experience. Not to mention the possible experience of actually feeling the heat and energy in your chest from your newly-freed radiating heart.

To further illustrate, imagine that all you knew was living in a dark cave and then one day an earthquake moves the rock covering the entrance to this shadowy place in which you have resided. Suddenly you experience light that you did not know was there. At first you experience this life-changing event physically. Next you reorient and register

*your awareness. Then you adapt and incorporate this new
light into your way of being.*

*This type of thing happens when you drop the energetic
barriers surrounding your heart.*

*You knew this lightness as a child, as does everyone. As
you grow and are programmed with beliefs about the
accepted behaviors of society, you slowly and unwittingly
begin to apply the energetic layers around your heart to
block what you perceive as injurious to your being. It is a
natural response and you are neither taught that it exists
nor instructed how to avoid the process.*

I'd like to experience this lightness you're describing and the
dropping of these heart walls. How would I go about doing something
like that? If I'm in the dark and don't know it and there's a better way
of being, you don't have to get my attention with an earthquake. Just
point and say 'fetch' and I'm on the way.

*You are being pointed in the direction of heart wall
removal. There are energies around you that are aware of
the modality. Set the intention and mention the term to
those you feel would understand. You will soon be
connected with a source that will be able to clear your
energies*

*We do not mean to appear unconcerned or vague. Ask
those around you about body code and emotion code. You
will find your way soon.*

Those that know how to clear this energy are before you.

BACK STAGE

At this point in the book-writing process, I had a side conversation with the energy that's assisting with this project. I present this side conversation as an example of the universe doing its connection process.

I didn't intend for this exchange to be in the book. I was just casually connecting on the side while I was sifting through some word placement concerns of the text. I wasn't tuned into anyone specific. That's why I used the term, 'energy,' below to indicate that I was connected with something not in my physical location. Later I thought that you the reader might find this exchange interesting.

Energy. *We like your title.*

Me. Which one?

Energy. *The one below.*

(I had written two title choices at the top of a page and they meant the second one that I had written down. I actually ended up using the first one.)

Me. Conferring with the Universe?

Energy. *Yes, it is catchy. It implies ongoing connection. That is what this is all about.*

Me. That makes sense.

Me. So did you guys give me that or did I do it all by my lonesome?

Energy. *You are the creator. Who do you think came up with it?*

Me. Interesting. I thought I was being divinely inspired.

Energy. *You were. You are divine, would you not say?*

Me. Yes, at least according to my book.

Energy. *You are truly divine and we are here to verify that. You are the one that creates, remember?*

Me. Well, yes, but I know I asked for help with a title and just thought I was heard and then it was given to me.

Energy. *It was a two-step process. Yes, you did ask for help, which is unlike you, and second you were heart-felt about wanting the help. You were sincere in your request with strong energy. That is all it took and then the universe processed the request. It went like this. This morning you thought of the first title and then later in the day you were inspired by another set of words that your being processed and mixed with the other words from this morning. Your mind assimilated the options. It was all part of a grand design. The title was in place already. Your heart just had to find it. The book was already titled and written before you started. You just found the title today. Rather exciting, would you not say?*

Me. Yes, I would say. It's one of those events that you want to have happen and when it does you're surprised that it really did.

MOTHERS DAY

My mother was an alcoholic. When I was little, there was quite a social pattern in which my parents participated. I remember liquor and beer always being a part of the environment. To me, that was what adults did. They drank some form of alcohol when they were together.

58

I never was exposed to falling-down drunken adults. And as far as I knew, it was always being consumed in the evening after work or at parties. My parents had a cocktail-after-dinner kind of thing and at gatherings on weekends. I was allowed to taste beer and wine at times when I asked. And during the holidays my brother and I were allowed to have a very small glass of a sweet wine. My mother's thought about this was to expose us to it and minimize the mystique.

As a kid I did like the way beer tasted. I never abused alcohol per se, although I'll admit to wanting to experience the effect of alcohol in high school. Then in college alcohol was definitely part of the scene. I got drinking out of my system in college and have never really been attracted to it other than a drink here or there.

Actually that's not correct; I am attracted to alcohol. I thoroughly enjoy a killer margarita. I think that's the best drink on the planet. It would be more accurate to say that after having been around my mother, I developed an attachment to all of my brain cells. Other than a few purposeful escapes from reality, I have gone without. The high has never lasted that long and I've never enjoyed the aftermath or recovery. Drinking didn't work for me the way it did for my mother. I remember telling her about that and her reply was that I didn't try hard enough.

I had college behind me and some military commitments out of the way and then got married. Shortly after that my parents divorced and that's when my mother's dependency took off with enthusiasm. It was quite an experience and growth opportunity, I must say.

I'd never had the experience of dealing with an alcoholic on any level and I didn't have any idea of what was ahead. By the time everything really got crazy with my mother, I was married and living in Arizona, while she was in California. I'd get these bizarre phone calls from her where she would go off on tangents about my brother and his family who lived in the same house with her.

She would basically slam everything he and his family did. Then the story would get repeated multiple times within the same conversation. During these calls my mother would conversationally pit me against my brother and vice versa. By the time I got off the phone with her, my stomach would be in a complete emotional knot and I'd be totally consumed with frustration and anger. It felt miserable.

In the aftermath of these calls, I'd be in a mental twist where I was conversing and arguing with my mother in my head. I'd run this mental loop, trying to create a logical verbal attack on my mother where I could reason with her, straighten her out, and win the confrontation. Then after having test-driven these all-consuming arguments in my head, I'd call her back and launch my plan to get her to see the light, only to realize that no matter how much I prepared mentally to debate with my mother, I'd still lose the skirmish. Every time! It got to the point where I'd lose the arguments with her in my head before I even tried the verbal version.

An alcoholic is very slippery, conversationally. About the time you think you have them cornered, they flip things around on you and you don't know what just happened. My heart would pound and I'd feel the frustration come up while I was trying to corral my mother. I'd get very worked up and feel so helpless because I couldn't get a handle on this mess with her. I couldn't solve anything. I couldn't get her to understand anything from my viewpoint. I'd hang up the phone totally disconcerted and lost. I never knew what to think or feel or do next. In the early stages of these encounters, I didn't know what I was dealing with – a person consumed burying their discomfort under alcohol. I didn't know that all the logic in the world wouldn't work on a person with a pickled brain. Their whole existence is consumed with justifying their position to maintain the consumption of the drug. You get circumvented on all levels and left in the dust.

At one point I went to California and made a surprise visit to my mother. I thought I'd just show up unannounced and see what the heck was going on. It was going to be a short fact-finding visit. OMG!

The day I got there, my mother was, of course, chagrined to see me on the door step. She was wearing some old thrift-store dress that was three sizes too big. She went into a demeanor of coy surprise and sheepishly tried to act as if everything was normal. Then she attempted to be welcoming as she was pulling at her oversized clothing, trying to keep it from falling off. The house was riddled with fleas. As I got further inside, I found an unkempt, dirty house and stacks of vodka bottles under the master bath vanity. And those were the high points. She knew why I was there. Her cover had been blown.

Initially I didn't know what to do. This behavior was all new to me. I didn't understand any of the performance that I was seeing. Our conversation was meaningless and I held back what I was thinking because it wasn't going to do any good. This woman was obviously not all there.

My tactic was going to be to back out the door slowly and leave gracefully, then swoop in from behind and solve the problem. I wanted to digest what I had encountered.

I was so naive.

Somehow with the help of my father's corporate insurance, he got her into a rehab situation. I don't remember how that happened because I was not involved. But I was glad about it. At least something was being done.

My father and brother didn't really know what to do for her. At first none of us did. Unwittingly what they did was more enabling than they realized. For instance, before a person comes home from rehab, you don't clean up the squalor they were living in to make everything nice. The right thing to do is leave it the way it was so when they arrive home, they can see what they created as a life style while they were in an alcoholic fog.

If the rehabbed person walks into a cleaned-up kitchen with no stacks of vodka bottles and carpets that have all the stains and dirt and fleas removed, then there's no reinforcement as to the depths that they had taken themselves. Instead they arrive home and walk in and mentally go into a 'what was the big deal?' state of mind. I think the one thing that did rattle my mother was the fact that when she was in rehab the first time, my dad had her two dogs put down. They were in poor physical condition and there was no one anywhere that could take them in. It was a practical move on my father's part.

Eventually, my mother was in and out of rehab over the years. She would go in and then come out a little wiser and then start drinking again. After her fourth or fifth crash, I somehow managed to get her in a half-way house recovery program here in Arizona.

Prior to that, however, I finally reached a point where I'd had enough and decided to take the bull by the horns. I tried to legally get control of my mother's estate in an effort to grab the cat by the back of the neck and get this whole alcohol thing fixed. This was going to be my final 'everything I have to give' attempt to repair the mess. I had to do this to clear my conscience and know that I had done all I could to help her. I was tired of the frustration and anger that I kept putting myself through, dealing with her and her addiction.

In the end, it all came down to a court hearing for me to become her executor and I was denied. The words of the judge were essentially that my mother needed to deal with her own demons; no one could do it for her. At the time in my 'let's get this thing under control' outlook, I didn't really appreciate the judge's decision. Let's say I wasn't expecting that verdict to come down. Damn, she slipped through my hands again.

I had been so sure that if I got control of her estate, then I could steer her and get her straightened out. I wasn't sure if I had won or lost that day. At first I thought I had lost. Who's to say? I learned a lot. After the legal judgment, I figured I could let go of the whole thing and relax. I had done all I knew to do.

Mom went back to California and was in and out of rehab several more times. To my aggravation, my brother, who lived near our mother, would keep showing up to find her passed out on the floor or on the verge of death and would get her back into the hospital and rehab. At one point, I remember telling my brother to stop going over there and just let her die. Nothing we were doing for her was making any difference. The last time she went under, I think it was the sixth time, the hospital called and asked me to attend some rehab process to support her in her recovery. I told the woman on the phone that I wasn't going to do that. I said that my attitude was if she wanted to kill herself then so be it – I was done.

In later years, my mother told me that after her last time hitting bottom, she came to and realized she wasn't going to drink any more.

And she didn't.

Mom became very active in Alcoholics Anonymous and had a lot of her own experiences over the years. Many I heard about repeatedly, when I'd see her. She didn't do well in the memory department, as far as recalling what she had and hadn't told me. It was very common to hear the same story several times in the same visit. Even in the same hour. My mother was quite the armchair philosopher after she sobered up. Not that she wasn't before. I'd hear her coaching other women in A.A. over the phone. Her approach was, "Do what I say, not what I've done."

Speaking of awareness, I recall a story my mother would relate when my brother and I were very young. She would talk about sitting at the dinner table as a kid with her father the doctor.

She would go into an endorphin state any time she spoke to my brother and me about her dad. She would get this glazed look on her face as she mentally went back and recalled past times of her childhood surrounding her father.

This story was about her dad sitting at the end of the dinner table with her twin brothers sitting to his left. One of the brothers said something that didn't set well with Granddad. Apparently with one fell swoop of his arm, my grandfather back-handed the nearest twin to the point of knocking him over backwards out of his chair.

The strange thing was this remembrance was always presented to my brother and me as a comical thing. I'm sure in reality it was not comical, but unnerving for any one sitting at the table that night. My brother and I'd laugh and want her to amuse us with other comical stories of her child hood. For some reason, this remembrance came up the most.

There was always a twist for me in her stories because what I haven't told you was that her father the doctor left my mother, aunt, two uncles, and my grandmother high and dry financially, never to look back. He remarried and got involved with narcotics by writing himself prescriptions until he finally got caught by the medical authorities. He went through some rehab in the day and was given his medical license back but couldn't prescribe narcotics after that. It's my understanding that at some point, however, he died of an overdose of something.

Now correlate this story with the adulation and adoration my mother had for her father – things didn't line up. In reality, Granddad was a little brutal and had an addictive personality. Of course, my mother didn't want to see her dad that way. Just on a whim one day I was with one of my uncles and I told him of my mother's adulation of her father. A really weird look came over his face hearing that. I don't recall his words and he didn't go into any detail, but my uncle's view of his father was not a match to my mother's version.

I was married with children the day my mother called to tell me about an A.A. moment. Somewhere in her healing process, she had an epiphany. Mom had called to tell me that she had been guided to realize that her dad, the man she'd had on a pedestal, wasn't really a very nice guy. Fireworks went off for her upon this realization. That conversation obviously put things better in line for me as well. It was a clearing moment, as it released that mental twist I had been carrying for a very long time.

I was sitting outside on our patio a few days after the Sedona book seminar, eating what was left of dinner after everyone took off to Boy Scouts and home work. The evening temperature was perfect. I was all alone and loving it. I started to think that this would be a good time for someone to magically pop in. It was quiet and I could concentrate on the intuitive conversation.

A few minutes later I received, "Your mother is here." That startled me a little because my mother had passed away over a year prior. So my reply was, "Okay. Why would she be here?" I was feeling neutral about such an encounter, not jubilant, and I wasn't sure what I was going to say. I could've unloaded on her, but why? If she had known how to do things differently then she would have. I hadn't been able to connect with her since her passing, which I found unusual. She just up and disappeared. Now I get, "She wants to talk to you."

So I took a deep breath and slowed my breathing. I put my attention to the upper right side of my head, going into right brain. As I tuned in, I did an emotion check. What do you say to your dead mother? I was curious about what was coming but not excited.

I had disconnected with her emotionally long ago. I did, however, out of respect, continue to be the dutiful son. But as she got older, she became less fun to be around. My brother had taken over her house and she lived in the converted garage. I had finally figured out that she played a two-sided game. She'd idolize me when I was talking to her and be negative about my brother and his family. Then she played the game in reverse when I wasn't there.

In preparation to connecting with mom, I went into my process and mentally pretended to put my left brain in a bed, put the blankets over it, and tucked it in. I do this to slow it down and let the right side take over. As I felt my right brain wake up, I created a mental image of my mother and simply thought of her name, got a mental snapshot, and went with that. This process put me on the other side.

Mom came into view. I could see that she had taken on the look of being in her late thirties or early forties with a shortened haircut and blondish hair. The next thing I was aware of was her talking.

> *I'm so glad I can talk to you. I just wanted to tell you how sorry I am for the way I treated you when you were growing up.*

As I guarded my emotions, I could see that she had very anxious body language. It was like someone might have if they were in a hurry to get words out before they forgot them. As she excitedly spoke, she and I took what I'd best describe as an imaginary seat on a bench; she was on my right. I asked her why she picked the age she was portraying. She said she had felt at her best energetically in her early forties.

Next, we talked about why I hadn't seen much of her since she passed. Her response was that she had a lot of stuff to work out. She went on to speak of having been an alcoholic, her father issues, and so on. For some reason, I recalled that she was never high maintenance.

She had smoked her whole life and liked to sit in the sun. While alive, her skin was definitely a product of her life style.

Something distracted me and there was a break in the action, so I came in the house. Then I heard, "Your mother is still here. She wants to convey to you how she feels." I wasn't sure who was buzzing in my brain.

When Gabe or someone shows up to connect, it's as if a person walks up to you from the side and leans around and puts their face directly in front of yours. In addition I sometimes get this little mental twist and a dizzy sensation that I've learned to be their knock on the door.

"Who is this?" I asked.

Gabe. I am your team leader, remember? Your mother is here to negotiate a deal with you. She wants to talk to you some more.

Interesting... I realized I was putting myself back into an emotionally guarded state.

Hi honey! I didn't know you were so good at this stuff. You can even see me when we do this talking.

Hi, Mom. Yes, it's pretty awesome. I found out how to do it in recent years. It was pretty exciting for me the first time I had confirmation I was actually on your side connecting. I'm still trying to come up with a way to take it to the bank. So what can I do for you, my dear mother?

You don't have to call me 'mother.' We are hardly that any more. But anyway how are you doing, sweetie?

I think I'm doing terrific. It looks like I might be able to get out of the plumbing business. I'm going to be a world-renowned author, you know. So maybe I can lay down the wrenches. I'm tired of climbing around attics and under houses and putting my hands where others would dare not, as it were. How are things with you, Mom?

I know we just spoke a little while ago while you were eating dinner. I wanted to talk to you so badly. I haven't been around much since I passed.

I've wondered about that. I figured you were off soul-searching or something. I wasn't sure.

I was. I just didn't know what to say to you until now. I wasn't ready then. Gabe found me and invited me to finally talk to you. I wanted to say how sorry I am for the life I led with you. While it was a pretty good life for us, I did some things I shouldn't have, as a mom. I wasn't the mom I meant to be, although I was doing the best I knew how.

I didn't mean to shell shock you like I did with the "should-ing." I never realized I did that so much. I wanted you to meet my standard so I kept the pressure on you. You were a good kid and I loved you very much. You were such a good kid that I never really had to do much except feed you. You were self-sufficient most of the time.

I never really knew how good I had it with you. Kyle, on the other hand, was a handful and I never really disconnected with him. I held on to him so I wouldn't be alone. I knew I couldn't do that with you. You were always so on the go. You never stopped. Always doing something and going here and going there to do who-knew-what. You couldn't sit still.

Anyway I wanted to thank you for all the help you were to me when I got divorced from your dad. You took over for a while. I knew that at the time and you took over again when I was crashing with the drinking. You never stopped trying to help until you saw that I had to figure things out. Then you let go and eventually I got it. Thank you for all the help you gave me. Kyle did his bit, too. You both managed to get me to the other side in your own way.

I didn't mean to end things with you and Kyle the way they went. I'm sorry for that. I should've been more into the planning of the estate. I didn't do what I was supposed to do. You know I loved you most.

Mom, when you used to do the 'I love you best' thing, I tried to never let that get into my head. I think you used to say things like that to whoever was in front of you at the time. I do know you loved me the best way you knew how, though.

And it's okay, Mom – I didn't know I was being abused. I didn't know the difference. I figured I'd cut my own path and you guys could do whatever and I'd just check in with you. Besides your parenting has given me a lot of ideas for a book. Maybe I can call it, "How to Let Your Parents Raise You and Love Them Anyway."

Thanks a lot, Scott. I love you, too.

I disconnected and started to write something else. Then I saw my mother turn to Gabe with body language, like, "Are we done?" I didn't realize I had disconnected so fast. I went back. "Sorry, Mom. Do you need more hugs?" I esoterically walked over to her and gave her a hug, which was 3-D to her and only third-eye visual to me.

I had better go now. You look like you are busy.

I mentally switched back to writing on another page of this book. As we unhugged, I said, "Thanks, Mom. I mean it, really… Thanks a lot. Now the least you could do is go get me the winning lottery numbers."

FATHER'S DAY

Having my mother enter this work, I have to give my father equal time. At this writing, he is still on the planet. My dad comes to mind when I see small airplanes fly overhead. He never took flying lessons but had been in small airplanes related to his corporate position, having to go here and there for meetings. My dad had no real love for small aircraft because whenever he had been in one, there was always a close call. It was like clockwork with his energy, I guess. On two occasions with my interest in flying, I had the chance to fly my dad somewhere. Both times it was in southern California. They were flights that had no purpose other than to just go flying with my dad and show him my stuff. And wouldn't you know, both times we went up, we had near mishaps.

Hi, Gabe. I wasn't expecting you.

Scott, I wanted to point out something you overlooked here.

But, of course, Gabe. Go right ahead. I'm waiting with bated breath to hear your take.

In your indifference to your father versus your connection with your grandfather, there was a huge gift for you that you received directly from your dad. You may have overlooked that for the most part. Your father modeled playing it straight. He never was a source of discord verbally toward anyone. He never really adulated anyone but you never heard him tear anyone apart from a critical point of view. He maintained a balance of neutrality on almost all subjects. That was the benefit for you. You were not double-teamed by two negative Nancy's, as it were. He was a great example in the sense of taking things as they appeared. Does that strike a chord within you?

I think I know what you mean. And yes, my dad never really complained about anything or anyone. If there was anything he got woeful about, it was the household spending. He would get mad out of nowhere and pound some fists on counters. This unfortunately is a behavior I have exhibited over the years, to my embarrassment.

Then Scott, maybe a lesson is being learned in your case. Keep working on the fist-pounding behavior. It does not serve you or anyone witnessing the behavior.

Yes, Gabe I'm very cognizant of that and am working on it. Besides, pounding your fists on things hurts.

After my Grandfather died, I tried to switch to my dad for a mentor. It just didn't work. My dad had certainly influenced me in some ways philosophically, but I soon realized again what I had forgotten, the recognition that my dad was not my grandfather. There wasn't much in him that I could to connect with.

He went with me to Arizona to get me set up for my first year of college. Our first night in Tempe, home of Arizona State University, we met some other new students at the hotel where we were staying and ended up taking them with us to a famous western-style restaurant in northeastern Phoenix. On the way to the restaurant, we got lost in an unpopulated desert area. It was late afternoon, it was August, and it was hot. My dad was driving, I was riding shotgun, and the new acquaintances were in the back seat. As we were finding our way, we came upon a car off to the right of the road with the hood up. There was a young man standing next to the non-functioning vehicle, obviously pondering his situation. I'm sure that when he saw us, he thought help had arrived.

My dad slowed to a stop so that I was immediately adjacent to the man. I rolled down my window, assuming we were going to offer assistance to this guy. My dad proceeded to ask him for directions to the western restaurant we were looking for. Strangely, he knew of it and offered directions all the while leaning on his car, in the middle of nowhere, with the hood up. My dad said thanks and proceeded to drive away, leaving this guy with the broken car in the middle of nowhere with no help! Being as this was before cell phones, it was a shock to me. I was dumbfounded that we weren't going to offer help and expressed that to my dad.

I tempered my reaction a little because of our new acquaintances in the back seat. My dad's reaction was to look in the rearview mirror and remain neutral about it. I interpreted his expression to mean, "And what's your point?" He didn't turn around. He went on down the road, following the directions. I remember looking back at the guy as he watched us drive away. I can tell you that he had a look of disbelief on his face. I was also in disbelief and embarrassed because I assumed the guys in the back seat were surprised that we didn't offer help. But then, maybe they weren't affected at all.

Fast forward to me being married with children. On several occasions, only because of my own need to replace my grandfather, I kept trying to go out of my way to see and connect with my dad. I even bought and delivered to him an artificial Christmas tree that I hauled from Phoenix to San Diego. My wife at the time ran into a really good deal on it and we were passing it on to my dad and his wife. I always was doing things like that trying to create a bond that just wasn't going to happen. Once I realized it was a pipe dream to emotionally connect with my dad, I started reducing the energy I put into trying to bond.

At some point after scaling back my efforts with my dad, he and his wife made a trip through Phoenix on their way to some destination north of Arizona to meet with friends. I remember finding out about it and being livid at the fact that at one point they were within 10 miles of where I lived but didn't let us know. I had a strong temptation to complain, "And you didn't even call or stop by to say 'Hi'? Seriously?" I guess the best description I could give is that I just wasn't feeling the love. I let myself grind on that for some time and then decided to call my father and lay into him.

There was just one problem with that idea. He didn't even flinch. All he said was, "You're mad at me." My heart started pounding at that one. What the heck am I supposed to do with that kind of response? At this encounter I finally learned that I was wanting him to be something he was never going to be.

I've heard it said that there's a gift in everything. If I apply that creed to the phone call where I was going to set my dad straight, then the gift would be that I realized I should just let it go. There was just nowhere for the emotional cords I was throwing toward my dad to take hold.

Scott, are you sure you want to stop here. There is more to tell.

Gabe, I'm scanning my memory banks and not landing on anything. Have you got any hints as to the direction I should be going?

Scott, why not dig a little deeper. There is a spot way down in the subterranean layers of your brain hiding behind some very dusty mental boxes. Take the lid off some of those boxes when you find them. It will be very clear to you which remembrance will apply here.

Gabe, I did some digging and I think I found it. It has to do with when my dad and I happened to cross paths at my grandparents' house. He was in Ohio on business and I was on my way back to Arizona after fulfilling some military requirements in Maryland.

That would be the one. In a sense, you were jolted with a dose of reality that you looked at as betrayal. It was a moment that hardened you a bit more emotionally. This experience deeply altered your perception and trust levels.

OK, THEN! I'm having a lot of resistance come up on having to look at this one.

As one would expect. It was a defining moment and you were not a kid. It shaped your relationship with your father from an adult perspective. It changed your outlook toward a man that you thought you knew. You took a step backwards and had to realign your view of this gentleman. It was an eye-opener on an adult level. It was a bout with the life experience. Go ahead, you can do it. You can reach in, reveal, digest, and come out on top with this one.

Gabe, I'm having a hard time dealing with this remembrance. I'm sort of surprised at myself.

It is one of those deep wounds that you have buried, my son. We encourage you to express this one. You will not falter. We are at your side.

Okay, I can do this!

THE DAWN ARRIVAL

On this occasion, my father and I had rendezvoused at my grandparents' farm in Ohio, as we were traveling related to some things going on in our lives. Since my dad was on corporate business, my mother was home in California.

This particular night on the farm, I was sleeping upstairs in the one spare bedroom at the southwest corner of my grandparents' house.

One window of the bedroom faced south; the other window allowed you to look to the west, and was in somewhat of an alcove that jutted outward from the exterior wall. From there, you could look toward town and see the fields on the west side of the farm. You also had a complete view of the tree-lined driveway from the house as it went west through the front yards and turned to the highway on the north side of the farm. As a kid, I had always enjoyed looking out this window. Especially early in the morning when the light was low and everything outside was casting shadows.

On this night my dad had to attend some sort of business meeting and he had not gotten back by the time my grandparents and I finally gave up waiting for him and went to bed. With only one spare room, he and I were bunking together and since he was not back yet I had the room to myself and settled in.

I slept soundly that night and just as the light of dawn was starting to increase, I woke up to a noise outside that was the unmistakable sound of a car moving on a gravel driveway. Because it was barely light I got up to look out the west window where the noise was coming from. In a wondering state of mind, I saw the car my dad had rented coming down the lane from the main road. Puzzled, I did one of those millisecond putting-two-and-two-together things. It's dawn, my grandparents are still asleep, and dad has not been home all night. What kind of business meeting lasts all night? Holy, what the…!

I didn't know how to feel. I was not clear on why I was seeing my out-of-town dad coming in at dawn from a business trip. I was in a shocked state and didn't know what I was going to ask or say to him. So I thought I'd play it safe and not say anything and see what happened next. Maybe the car just broke down. Yeah, right.

I got back in bed and heard the car continue up the drive and then listened as I heard my dad come in the house and upstairs. He was doing the tip-toe approach and I acted like I was asleep. He got undressed and went to sleep on the spare cot. I, of course, was wide awake with my mind reeling trying to come up with logical explanations for what all this meant. He was Mr. Play-It-Straight. At least that's what I thought. My existing perception of Camelot had just been shaken.

I never did bring up the subject to my dad. And he never said, "Gee, guess what happened to me last night. You're never going to believe it. Did you hear me coming in early this morning?" To me, his lack of engagement on the situation confirmed my suspicions. I kept all my feelings to myself and never told anyone about my sense of his departure from, let's say, integrity. I did place my dad in a different category of respect, however. I guardedly downgraded his rating in my world.

This all put me in a tough spot emotionally. I wasn't a kid anymore and knew that people do what people do, but at the same time this was my dad. He was not supposed to do what other people do. But he did. I never had any closure on the experience. I never had any proof of anything one way or the other – only questions to which I didn't want answers. Even if I had the chance to ask, I don't know if I would.

It's funny as I relate this happening, I can feel the emotions surrounding my confusion, suspicions, and disillusionment of the moment. I can still see the rental car coming down the drive in the early morning light wondering what to do next. So what do I do next?

I realize my dad didn't do anything to me. I don't really know what he was doing or with whom that night. I personally had no cuts or bruises related to the incident. My wounds from this experience were totally emotional.

The odd thing is any pain I felt was of my own making. I didn't come up with that realization for a number of years. I just carried the self-inflicted wound around inside. My dad having come in at that time of morning was certainly out of character, but just another event in all reality. It was just something in my father's life that I happened to witness. I created the righteous sense of blame and injustice about my perception of what I observed. He simply came back to the house very early one morning in a rental car. I had the option of attaching any conclusion and related emotion to it that I wanted. Then I had the opportunity of experiencing the feelings associated with the emotion I chose. I guess it was an either/or kind of thing. Not knowing any better, I went with the pain option rather than maintaining my joy. In fact I went with the pain option for quite a long time.

Gabe, if you want to pop in here that would be fine. I'm feeling a little lost as to where to go with this section. Earth to Gabe. Earth to Gabe. Come in, Gabe.

We were waiting for you to come up with your own synopsis of the situation. We knew you had it in you. You did very well piecing together all the parts of the experience. It took you some time to come up with the realizations, but in the end you put everything on paper very nicely. Our only addition would be a few comments that we will cheerfully relay to you.

There were many gifts for you in this life experience. You got to see your father in a different light. It changed your relationship with him in a way. Who is to say if it was better or worse? That is for you to determine.

What we want to make note of here is that in any given situation, you can make yourself miserable or you can go to higher elevations of thought and simply observe and stay neutral and pain-free. Do you understand?

The high point for you, and anyone else experiencing these words, is your awareness that the emotional pain or pleasure you personally perceive from any given happening is caused by you, the driver of the bus. You are clear now of your own mental brutality against yourself as a result of how you look at and react to given happenings. That is quite a huge hurdle to get yourself over.

Our encouragement for you is to keep practicing the art. You did a fine job of presenting that awareness and many will relate and elevate themselves as a result.

Thank you. I felt I was floundering through the whole thing. I kept wondering why you weren't grabbing the reins, as it were.

This was your story. You had to digest it and present it. It would not have benefitted you for us to tell you where to go with this rendition. We know it was difficult for you, but once again we applaud your tenacity.

Section III

No one saves us but ourselves.
No one can and no one may.
We ourselves must walk the path.

Buddha

WHERE DOES THE SKY END?

As a kid in the country I had lots of opportunity to see clouds and blue sky. I was watching the sky one day and started to wonder where it stopped. I didn't know it at the time, but I was in the process of creating another defining moment with that thought. You'd think that after the Santa realization, I'd have learned. But no, I had to ask my mother yet another question about what is.

She and I were near our front porch on a spring day doing the mom-kid thing outside. I don't know what triggered it, but the question took over my focus.

"Mom, where does the sky end?" She casually answered, "It doesn't end. It goes on forever."

My little brain didn't like that. I became disconcerted with that answer. I wanted things to be black and white, and 'going on forever' was not in that category. It's sort of like the mathematical formula for the ratio of a circle's circumference to its diameter. That number has no ending, so you end up rounding off pi at 3.14. Only you can't round off forever. I was surprised at the answer. I had no frame of reference and it scared me. I didn't know what to do with the information and didn't want the sky to go on forever because that meant that no matter what I did, I couldn't see the conclusion. I like to see how the story ends. I was uncomfortable just being left to hang out there in this philosophical and mathematical void.

I mention this experience because it was a profound door-opener for me, in that it was the beginning of intellectual ponderings that I still have today. It's the 'inquiring minds want to know' kind of thing. A lot of the time I still don't know what to do with the answers I get. At times I categorically, flat-out don't like the answers that show up.

I just had a thought. Now that I think about it, when I get answers that I do like, it's sort of boring because there's nowhere to go conversationally or intellectually. When everyone is in agreement, all there is to do is sit around and rehash the events that led up to everyone agreeing. So maybe getting answers I don't like is better because then there's something to roll around in my head and chew on. Okay, I'll go with that. Answers I don't like are a good thing. I hadn't considered that side of the coin before.

Hi, Gabe. I thought that was you buzzing around.

Scott. As some might say, what is happening? It is important for you to see who you are here. You are not a child any longer and you need to view this experience from a different perspective.

Okay.

If you look at this experience through the eyes of an adult and not from the perspective of a child, there is a different perspective available for your viewing. A child sees things differently because there is no foundation or reference point for the young mind to measure against. The perspective of a child is such that it is forming a yard stick with such questions. Also the child is simply qualifying its environment. The child mind needs to create a structure, of sorts, to assemble a mental picture of how it perceives things to work. Do you understand?

Yes, I follow you. Go on, I'm listening.

Your picture of who you are at this moment differs from your perception of who you were as a child. Is that clear? Are you following?

Yes, that makes sense.

Next, you have to see yourself as having a way to maneuver through the questioning. Your concerns at the moment about infinity are different than your concerns when you first dealt with the concept. As a child you had no measuring stick to apply to the subject to help you find balance in your developing conceptual center. Be gentle with yourself and with your memories.

Do not bash those around you, in the sense that they did not understand you, as such. Remember that an adult has lost the ability in most cases to accurately see through a child's eyes. They are wearing different glasses and it is difficult for adults to see where the child mind is. Adult measuring devices are calibrated at a different scale. So try as they might, an adult will find it difficult to convey accurately at a child's level.

The relevance of what I have just said is that conceptually you were developing your devices for measuring your life's perspective. So for the most part it was simply a step for you in the process of leaving childhood and moving up the ladder to the next level. If you can see your life as a steady process of moving up the ladder of thought, rather than a shocking horrific experience, the pain is lessened or neutralized over the event.

So, Gabe, if I understand you right, you're saying that everything that takes place is just an event. Maybe the event takes you up the ladder or it takes you sideways but in either situation it's to be recognized as just an event. And if everything is just an event, I get to choose how I'm going to react to it. I can get aggravated and angered at a situation, or I can get wide-eyed with excitement over what I've just experienced. I think you're suggesting I stay emotionally neutral. Is that what you mean?

Yes, all of that is what we want you to see, but only be emotionally neutral if you want to have that experience. That, opposed to excited or pensive or heart-felt and so on. To use your words, you will have to chew on this a while until it settles in. But you are on the right track of seeing the happenstance of the concept.

Remember to not be resentful of the childhood memories or the adults that you perceive as having tainted them. Every childhood memory you recall is a step in an upward direction emotionally and developmentally. View it all as a process, not an inquisition.

Okay, I'll try and work on that perspective.

FALLING FROM CLOUD 9

I had worked hard, owned my own business, raised my kids, pursued personal and intuitive development, and I couldn't do the marriage any longer. After 23 years, I had to call it quits. No harm, no foul. It just wasn't fun for me anymore. The short version is I just wanted out. I didn't want so much as a fork. I took the rental house and she got the castle. It was a hard decision for me because I'm not one to give up. It took me five years to actually make the move. Then one day in the entry way of the house as my wife was heading out the door to go exercise, I just blurted out, "I want a divorce," and life as I had known it turned on a dime. I wanted out so badly that in the end I ran to the point of selling my existing plumbing business. I didn't know what I was going to do. But I figured something would show up and I'd survive somehow.

Ultimately, I ended up in a relationship which developed as a result of attending a weekly personal development class run by a career psychologist. It was heavily attended on Friday nights and if you were a regular goer, you soon got to know everyone's stuff.

At this weekly group encounter, there was another attendee that I got to know. His name was Dennis. Dennis was a regular and I got to know his stuff, as he did mine. I learned that Dennis had a passion for dealing in the stock market. With the age of computers, you could sit at home, and buy and sell stocks on your own. It was sort of a hobby to him.

One day he had a brilliant idea and presented it to me. Basically it was to let him put some of my money in with some of his money, along with some money of other people. He would put it all in the stock market. Since the dollar amount of the group would be bigger than the individuals playing separately, there could be bigger moves, we would make more money, and it would all be split.

I never shirk from an opportunity. Sounds great to me!

While I was running away from my marriage, I also ran from plumbing and sold my business to an employee. So I had no job but a little cash. Okay, maybe this stock thing would be my new life!

The totality of the experience could well be the subject of its own book. Dennis truly believed what he was doing was working. Things got very out of hand in terms of the money that he was handling and the number of people who got involved in the opportunity. To his credit, Dennis encouraged others to learn what he was doing and his trading was an open book.

With divorce in hand and looking for new ways of supporting myself, I got interested in what Dennis was doing and started looking over his shoulder to learn what his process was. As I sat with Dennis, I noticed his method was skewed. Dennis, either through not wanting to see or not being aware, was misconstruing part of his trading process and basically was not making the profits that he thought he was. By the time I saw that he didn't know what he was doing, I had opened my own accounts and had what money I could muster in play. Toward the end of the stock-trading experience with Dennis at the key board of my computer, at one point I saw $29,000 of my last dollars disappear in a matter of 15 seconds. That was the remainder of most of the money I had received from the sale of my first plumbing business. Others took a big hit as well. Ouch! Okay, lessons learned, I guess.

The end result was I had no way to make a living. The woman I had met in group and I tried to do day trading in the stock market and what we didn't lose with Dennis we ultimately lost ourselves. I ended up living off credit cards to the tune of $100K and a car that I couldn't afford got repossessed. I was at the lowest financial point I had been since adolescence. Only when I was young, I was on my way up the ladder. Now I had fallen off the ladder and hit the dirt. Okay, I'm sure there's a lesson here somewhere.

The road back from there to here has had some interesting turns and a few bumps. I guess this is where I have to view all that happened as just a chain of events. That's right, just stay neutral. I have to say I sure learned a lot. Gabe, I feel you here.

Scott, I was pondering the way you told about your departure from your marriage to include falling to the ground. It is not always possible to see what the benefit of misfortune is until you look back at it. If you had just let the events take place and stayed in a neutral state, it would have been less demanding on you emotionally. You did push back and you did fight to dislodge your discomfort. But if you remember, nothing took you out of the opportunity the universe had for you to learn. You were not going to be permitted to move on until you went through the experience you signed up for. Yes, you signed up. It went perfectly. You should share the story of the message your significant other received about the job you saw in the newspaper.

Okay, I can do that. It just seems a little strange to tell that story here.

As Gabe mentioned, I did fight back. I'm not one to sit around and let things just happen. I do whatever I can to get and keep the ball rolling.

By the time the experience I'm about to relay took place, I had moved in with the woman I had met at the Friday night group. I felt I'd had enough of waiting for the universe to work things out. I was somewhere between the ground and the first rung of the ladder on the way to getting a life back. Early one morning I went out and picked up a want-ads listing of jobs. I got back to the house and went in to the kitchen table and started going through the columns.

My other half was up when I got back and enjoying the quiet before her kids woke up. I was scanning the paper looking to see what was out there for possible income. My eyes were drawn to a trade column wanting a foreman to manage crews that would be digging pipeline trenches. I was very familiar with that process and I can say categorically that I just knew that that job was mine – all I had to do was make the call and apply. I just knew it! I told this to my other half.

I could see her shift into her analytical mode and she decided then to go take a shower and left me to my knowing.

There I sat. Now I was in a tug of war with myself. If I took the job I'd be working for and having to answer to someone else's time frame. Having been self-employed, I discovered that I make a terrible employee. I'm too independent and I like being turned loose and don't want to have to report back. Just give me the job and let me go. Oh, and don't watch me. On the other hand, it would be a job. These credit cards I was living on weren't going to last forever. But taking the job would mean I'd be going right back into what I really wanted to get away from, only worse. But it was a job, we could have used the money, and it would stop the downhill slide. But... But... Back and forth went the mental gyrations.

It was still early when my new love came back into the kitchen with wet hair after her shower. The kids were still asleep. I was still pondering and going over the ads and grinding mentally about what to do. She was still in her deep analytical state and started to tell me about the epiphany she'd had while taking her shower. The awareness she had was that if I took this pipeline job, she and I'd be done.

In my brain what hit was, "What the heck are you talking about?" I thought that being proactive and working and bringing in an income was a good thing. She went on to explain that just as I knew the job was mine for the taking, she knew that if I did take the job it would alter the path that she and I were on and that we would be over as a couple. Of course, she didn't know where that all came from; she didn't know what the course was or what it would be. She was just sure that we would be finished.

Ahummm. Okay. I was not sure what to do with all of that. The funny thing was, I knew she was right. Not being one to generate bad karma, I thought okay, maybe there's something to this universe stuff and as much as I wanted to relieve the debt, I didn't go for the job.

I now know, looking back, that the income of the job would have diluted or altered our relationship to where we wouldn't have been put into the situations that we did go through. It would have delayed personal growth that wouldn't have taken place if there had been reduced pressure financially. We wouldn't have looked in directions that we ultimately considered.

Scott, that was a pivotal moment for you. You truly do not know how pivotal it was for you to not take the job. You were free to choose and logically you should have taken the job just for the job's sake. The universe spoke to you through your other half and you responded. Had you gone against your instincts and pursued the logical course, you would have made a turn on the road that would have taken you in a direction away from massive growth on a personal and soul level. You did not want to postpone your mission, so you wisely took the road less traveled. In this sense, the deviation from the norm and prudent action served you in a much greater sense than you can really know.

The truly amazing thing is you had the courage to face the decision that the universe preferred you to make. You were given an opportunity by the heavens to take the easy way out. But you did not. You courageously faced the challenge, even though you did not know what the challenge looked like. That was instinct at its finest. That was intuitive flow in full force. That was the universe doing its job and presenting you with a test that you set up for yourself, to find out who you really are. If you had taken the job, your course would have been altered and the process that you subsequently went through would have merely been postponed – postponed to maybe another life or another relationship.

The universe went through a lot of orchestration to set up that scenario for you, at your request, to explore. You took the right road. If you had taken the job, that would have been the right road also. Do you see? Simply put, the universe would have said, "Okay, let us set that up again and see if he goes for it this time." And you would have had it to consider all over again.

Gabe, I remember thinking, after the shower awareness, "Well I'm here on the planet now and I don't want to have to do this life over so let's see what happens."

It was a wise choice. You were tuned in, my friend. Tuned in is good. You did a skillful job of capturing a rather complex and intriguing journey from one life to another. You need to see yourself here as the conquering hero, not the fleeced sheep. You must remember you were part of the scenario by choice, as I recall. You gave the game your full attention, as you are giving this book your total energy. That is to say, you invited the experience into your life with vim and vigor. No one forced you to play as hard as you did. The events did not turn out as you had hoped.

But you are wiser and stronger for the experience. You showed up with all the intention you could muster. Your aim was at the stars. There is no dishonor in that. The dishonor would have been to not play at all and hide in a corner of your life. You lived dangerously on the edge, where few would dare to tread. You are greater for the experience. Had you played it safe, you would not be the person with the awareness that you have now and your talents of connection would not be as well honed. So pat yourself on the back for a job well done.

Thank you, Gabe, for giving me that perspective to consider. Yes, I did give it all I had. And I did learn a lot about myself. It's much easier to apply that thinking now some time after the event. At the time let's say I was not as understanding of the philosophical view that you're presenting now.

There is no substitute for experience. You did well to see who you were. You did not know at the time how in depth your exposure to self would be. You came out all the better for it and truly you became more enlightened. Without the experience you would not be who you are now and you would not be as effective at relating to others who might be in similar life challenges. So be proud of who you are. Do not foster regrets about the past. Embrace who you are and know that all is well. There is no continuum that you have to be in parallel with. There is no measuring stick that you have to align yourself against. Simply experience, evaluate, and replay. That is all there is for you to do in this life. It is a cycle that plays out on a continuum each day for each soul. There are many twists and turns in the road. But that is what you signed up for. Remember that! Please!

Okay, let my mind work on all of that for a while.

THIS IS THE GAME

Scott, there is a game that you get to participate in everyday and you have tickets for front-row seats. This game is so amazing it even gives you, the player, options to choose as to how it will turn out. It is, of course, the game of life. Options in the game include wallowing in misery, basking in an uplifted grateful mental state, or doing something somewhere in between. The game of life is like deciding if you want chocolate or vanilla. It is that easy. That is what most forget. This is being said because even in the realm of existence that we operate in, we are also trying to perfect our brightness. We strive to increase our awareness of being, just as we mentor you to do.

We mention state of being here because it is important to know that every waking and sleeping moment you have is a state of being. You ride a roller-coaster of emotions throughout your day, highly unaware of who you are or who you are being because you are more focused on the individuals outside of you rather than focused on the being that is you.

Be selfish for a change. It is okay. We give you permission. You should focus on yourself more often, as it were. Not to the point of rude possessiveness or harm to others, but with subtle awareness of who you are being at any moment.

You spend time in your workday perfecting your tasks at hand. We feel that the most important task is you. Learn to be conscious of what you think, feel, taste, and say. You are conscious of when you are thirsty or hungry. All you need to do is add in awareness of what you are thinking or feeling. Get lost in the project of you. You are probably thinking that does not really seem appealing. It is much more distracting to focus on others outside of yourself.

The true mission of life is often misrepresented from one generation to another. The mission at hand is you. You are the only one that matters in your world. That is not to say that greed and total consuming concern for self is the optimal way to be. One can certainly choose that experience until it proves to no longer be of benefit to the being at hand. And that will happen. A chosen action will give way, eventually, to another chosen behavior. It could take several lifetimes or it could take several seconds to decide that in a given moment, it is no longer pleasing or beneficial to remain who you are.

Moments will occur when you decide that you need an upgrade in beingness. The universe will support you, no matter who you choose to be or how long you choose to be who you are. As life experience presents opportunities to upgrade, remind yourself to not be discouraged by the past.

There are many interactions taking place within you now. Do not let events of the past cause you to think that you are 'less than.' Do not feel that somehow you missed the boat. The simple truth is you were not supposed to be on that boat at that time. There is still time to get on board; another will come around again. It may not be exactly the same boat but it will carry you on your journey just the same.

SPARKS

Scott, while you are waiting at the dock with ticket in hand, consider this. When you see a person walking down the street, they are on the street they chose to be on long ago. You have to remember that you also chose to be on this same street at this time long ago.

In some finite process, that person you are observing at any given moment was once a spark of energy that wanted to expand its universe just like you. It asked politely as you did and it was granted all its wishes.

When the event of expansion took place, this little spark was propelled into a physical universe so vast that it was startled at the grandeur it had asked for. It took a deep breath and jumped in with both feet. This little tiny ball of energy was astonished by what it saw through new-found eyes. It heard through new ears and touched and felt with new skin. It compiled all the sensations at hand, trying to make sense of who it was and what was happening.

It did not question its existence. It did not even question where it was. It just wanted to experience. And in the experience, it was not going to challenge its existence. It was too amused tuning into its sensory delights. There were opportunities ahead to discover and share with other sparks. There were challenges to be met. There were aspirations to peruse and dreams to chase.

This transformed spark, of course, encountered hurdles and a fog of doubt that started to dull the process of life experience. The little spark had to be reminded that the challenges in its new existence came with the request for life and that they were there to help it understand who it was.

If you were to know a life of no hurdles, you would have a life with no growth. There is not much to be said about a life without challenges and disappointments. There are no stories of victory to share, only stories of regret. When regret takes place, there is pain and longing to take different steps next time. Do not wait to take steps next time; take a step NOW! For now is all you have, my dears. We applaud your tenacity. We applaud your rhetoric. We applaud your teachings and misunderstandings. We applaud your ways of being and we applaud your moments of sadness. We even applaud your resistance to what is. For that all makes up the grandeur of life. We love the life you live. We love the life you could live, if that is what you want to do.

We are with you every step of the way, my loves. We applaud your fears. We applaud your contempt. We applaud your ways of doing something backwards just to see if you can. We applaud your malfunctions, whatever they may be. You can do no wrong. There is a grand game to play and the important thing for you to know is that you signed up for it. You put your name on the dotted line and pledged your soul to partake in this Grand Game. It is grand and all you can do is play it. Play it to the best of your ability. There are no losers. In this game of life, there are only winners. There are only those who wish to play.

Everyone near you, at any given time, entered the course and said to the universe, "I want to play a round." The universe said, "Hmmmm. Are you sure you want to do this?" They answered, "YES WE DO!" They did not hesitate; they did not blink. They only asked, "Which way do we go?"

Our offer to you is to know, dear ones, that you signed up for this life with UNBRIDLED enthusiasm. 'Unbridled' is an understatement, by all counts. It is not mandatory to be here. It is not a tour of duty against your will. You were applicant, accessor, and grantor in the process of acquiring the life that you now hold in your hand. It is a grand game that only you can play. No one, and we mean no one, can play it your way. To emulate another life is impossible.

So, my darlings, take to heart what we have said here.

Take to heart who you are being in this grand life. It is truly grand, you know. Take to heart that you hold the key in your hand at all times. No one else can put the key in the ignition and start it. That is impossible. Even the person who seems to be living a most unappealing life on some level asked to be invited into the game at that exact level.

As you requested, your life came with all the accoutrements you outlined. Do not be discouraged by the situation you are now experiencing. The life you are living right now, down to the smallest detail, is the life you ordered. The daily experience that you now have is the result of the request that you gave to the universe. Your experience at this very moment is the direct result of your submitted plan. Look how far you have come from being that little spark that just wanted to experience. Look how much you have accomplished on the scale of life. It took guts to step up to the plate and say, "I want to experience."

Knowing this can be disconcerting to some, we know, because that shifts the blame, or shall we say responsibility, of who you are to YOU. Do not be alarmed about who you are. You got what you asked for. You have not seen the best or the worst yet. You have simply seen what the result of your asking was.

That is quite a concept to grasp when those around you and near you display a tendency to victimize and blame others for their situation. Do not accuse, lest you be accused, as they say. The time is now to understand who you are. How do we know this is your time? Because you were drawn to and are reading these words!

This is our wish for you. Go forth and see what there is to see. Experience what there is to experience. Elevate from spark to inferno.

That's me. Look out, I'm on my way to being hot!

STOPPING THE UNIVERSE

Nothing stops personal expansion like the mental processes of the individual. The process of stopping the universe takes place in the mind, right there between your ears. Nothing encapsulates and hinders the process of the universe as much as the mind. The mind is the most powerful force that is.

Start to connect with who you are by seeing the world in a different way than you have. Do not see the world as adversarial. It is much better to see it as an opportunity to learn who you are. It is not as distant as you might perceive.

View your existence as a box. Boxes come with a lid or without. The box with no lid cannot be turned upside down, because then the contents will fall out. It must be kept upright. It is always open to allow anything that might happen by to fall in. In the case of a box with a lid, nothing new can enter the box and the lid keeps the contents locked away and safe.

You choose to either exist in a closed box or one that has the lid removed. A third option is to sometimes have the lid off and at other times have the lid on. A life with the lid kept in place tends to keep the contents safe at all costs. A disadvantage of living a life with the lid in place is that the life inside, as well as the lives outside of the box, miss out on the opportunity to connect with each other. No one else realizes what is in the box, for lack of viewing.

You must open your box and show others what is inside, hidden away safe and sound. There really is not any place that is totally safe and sound, however. There is only existence in a closed box or an open one. In the closed box, less will be experienced and what is felt or seen in the box is slight compared to an open-box experience. Being in the box with no lid is much more invigorating and memorable to the soul.

Our wish for you is to not be the one in the closed box. Be sure you are the one in the open box so that what is encountered is vibrant and indelible to the soul. The actions experienced inside the closed box are muted and less penetrating to the soul. Having said that, we encourage you to seat yourself at the front of the class and keep the lid open on the box called 'your life.'

Gabe, I have to ask a question here. I'm seeing a trend in what you're conveying to me. In several ways, you have implied that we create our own experience. I can choose to live in a box with a lid on it to minimize my exposure or I can live in an open box that will allow more events to show themselves. So if I allow a relationship with anyone or anything to come into my box, are you saying that I have created it? It sounds like no matter what situation I get into, it's my fault.

There has to be clarity added to your understanding here. There is no fault on anyone's part, just preparation for the next experience. That is to say you are not a trouble-maker. You are a spirit in form looking to see who you can be next. There are no bad guys here. You have to understand that. In the scheme of things, be aware that you have drawn yourself into an opportunity to find out what your strengths and weaknesses are. Do you see? There is not a road map in place, only tendencies on your part to put your physical self into a situation called life that will propel your spirit into a realm of greater understanding.

There is no greater classroom for you to be privileged to partake of. The teacher in the life classroom is the only variable. But in the whole scheme, there is no particular teacher. There are only life situations and relationships that become your teacher.

The opportunity to grow is only amazing or horrible, depending on how you look at it. It is not supposed to be hard. Some of you may recoil at that thought. But here again you have a situation being presented to you for your growing pleasure or your pain. You can accept any situation you are in as being a grueling effort or pleasurable experience. It is your choice. Do you not see how everything you do is created by your process of being here to experience? You choose your destiny. Your parents were no accident. When you think you were born into the wrong family or that you must have been switched at the hospital, think again. You walked up to the order counter and said, "I want a life, please. I would like to have two parents and an aunt with a loving nature with a side of grandparents that will be supportive and a brother that will be a nemesis to me to keep me on my toes."

You also could have walked up to the counter and said, "I would like a helping of third-world experience. Could you give that to me with a grass and mud hut with no modern conveniences?"

Another scenario might look like this – "Do you have any lives available where I can be a celebrity? I would like that to go with many relationships, please."

Do you see how this works?

Gabe, I'm trying to get my brain around the idea that I picked my parents or a marriage that wasn't all fun and games. I don't understand why I would've created some of the situations in my life that were the pits, as it were, just so I could experience being in the pits. I have to say that doesn't make sense to me.

Why would I create physical hardships or cancer or heart attacks? Why would I or anyone else choose a life in a third-world country where they would be dirt poor or live where they were in physical danger every day? Who would do such a thing? And why?

Scott, there are many aspects of your question to consider. First do not be concerned with the events in a life as being painful. They are only events to be viewed as either hard or frustrating or glorious and uplifting. These events need to be perceived as having potential to lead to other events that again can be viewed as hurtful or engaging. While you are deciding which views to take toward the events in your life, remember that you have to get away from the good-or-evil concept. There is really no good or evil to measure. There is only response.

Any event generates a reactive energy within you, whether you are aware of it or not. When you pay attention to the energetic responses you are generating, you will begin to see a trend in how you are responding to life. You have choices here. Keep generating the same internal energies or decide to reshape what you are energetically experiencing and trade it in for a different way of feeling. This is part of finding out who you are.

Gabe, but why would I order a life of poverty and pain versus a life of wealth and comfort? That just seems crazy. To me the choice would be that everyone would choose wealth and comfort. Why would you choose anything else?

Here, Scott. Maybe an example will help. Suppose Joe got married. He had children, then experienced divorce. Suppose Joe remarried a second and third time only to divorce again. Suppose that sometime after the third marriage, Joe was introduced to yet another woman. Now Joe goes on a first date with her and he realizes that this woman's personality is just like the personalities of the last three women that he married. Only on this encounter, Joe finally sees his pattern of choosing and realizes that this personality is not a good choice for him.

Obviously there was a pattern that was not healthy for Joe to continue creating and on the fourth encounter, he recognized that fact. The universe simply gave him four opportunities and he finally got things to click on the fourth try. These encounters in marriage for this individual were all in one lifetime. It could easily have been stretched out over four lifetimes. It just took him four encounters to become aware. He simply chose a life where he learned what he needed to learn and it took three marriages to learn it.

As for why one would choose to exist in a third-world country, only the soul knows. One environment might be more conducive to a particular soul goal than another. Each environment has its opportunities.

Just a side note for you to chew on – regarding wealth versus seemingly impoverished life styles, a person in a third-world country could very possibly have an elevated soul that sees the value in a simpler, more care-free life, where the pressures of accumulating wealth are not an issue. They may have mastered the process of thinking everything is glorious and uplifting.

You got me on that last thought, Gabe. I'm a little chagrinned at my thinking that wealth and comfort are the only way to go. So I guess that was a gift, of sorts, to see.

Be careful, Scott, your evolution is showing.

Gabe, going back to Joe, are you saying that he ordered a life where he said, "Just let me keep encountering the same bad connections until I realize that they aren't good for me."

Something like that.

I don't get it. So you say that we set up all these scenarios or situations in our life ahead of time on purpose and then we willingly get born and jump into the game just to learn from them?

Essentially.

Gabe, who the heck thought that one up?

Scott, it is the way of the universe. It is simple, but effective and very engaging. Ahh! Notice the word 'engaging.' That is the key word. To learn something by happenstance is the most effective way to etch it in your beingness. Does this make sense to you, my son? If you are simply presented with a concept, you do not truly absorb it until you experience it in depth on a personal level. Truly, it is a magnificent process. Every living being of consciousness is included in the process. There are no shortcuts.

Wow, do I feel silly. Here I was trying to be smart about living my life and avoiding pitfalls only to find out that I built in snares and booby traps into my existence, just to set up challenges for myself.

And indeed you did, with great style. Any action that you take in your life was in some sense preconceived. Not to say that you are strictly being controlled. You have many courses that you can follow but for the most part the trend of your life is forecast by you. Do you see?

Let's just say that I'm trying to get the vision incorporated into my thinking. Or in other words, I'm working on it.

WHY ARE YOU HERE?

Okay, I have my meditation music on. I'm settling down the left brain. I'm taking deep breaths exhaling with vigor and letting the air go. I can feel my being start to relax and shift into receive mode. I visualize taking my left brain out of my head and gently putting it to bed, like tucking a child in at night; I must slow down left brain. There I am. My eyes are closed and I'm wide awake in right brain. I hear, "Come and see us." Okay. I go to the third-eye vision center. I'm projecting a mental image of myself on their side. There they are. Gabe and the gang. They wave at me and mentally I return the gesture. I'm glad to connect after a long day. I become aware of Gabe's query.

Why are you here, Scott?

Do you mean with you on your side or on the planet Earth?

On the planet, but here with us. Why are you here with us? Why did you seek us?

I'd had a long day and was anxious to connect. I wanted to touch base before I went to bed.

That is not entirely true. You are here because we love you.

My brain is going to, "That doesn't make any sense."

You are here because you know we love you and it feels good energetically to be in our presence. That, my friend, is why you are here. You know, on some level, you will be adulated or instructed, in a sense. You are comfortable having us to communicate with and take you away from your Earthly life for a little while. Do you understand?

I'd have to agree with that. It's always nice to go where you expect to be loved or adored or congratulated. It's sort of like that saying, "You want to go where everyone knows your name." It's comfortable to come over to your side. And I know it's safe to go there. It's like my grandmother's attic. I don't know what I might find of my history or future.

Scott, you are right. Our attic is full of surprises. So what have you uncovered in the attic so far?

Do you mean on this particular occasion or in general?

During this session.

What is registering for me is I think that like energy attracts. Does that sound right?

There is more to it than that. You are attracted to this realm because it is home to you. You feel innately comfortable with our energy and wish to be here because it is the place where you think you can find answers. You continually reach to us for direction.

Gabe, I'm starting to feel like I'm in trouble. There's one of my little inner kids starting to come up like he got caught with his hand in the cookie jar.

Not to worry, Scott; we are not scolding you. We are just trying to guide you into some clarity here. You come to see us on a regular basis. Moments like these are more pronounced than you might suspect.

Gabe, I'm confused. I get that I'm drawn to you for my own connection experience. So is that okay or not okay – or are you wanting me to do something else?

Scott, we want you to be aware. There is something that we want you to see, in the sense that we want you to know why you are taking a particular action.

Give me a minute here, Gabe. I'm mentally scanning. The thought that I just had is that I'm looking outside of myself for answers.

That would be it, Scott. Do you see what you are doing? You are coming to us, hoping to have us issue you directions or guidance to situations that you ultimately find the answers for on your own.

So Gabe, I have to ask, is that a bad thing? Am I being uninvited?

No, Scott, you are not being uninvited and remember that there is no bad or good, only experiences of your choosing.

Okay, Gabe, the experience I'm choosing is to come over to your side and connect to the extent I can and get philosophical influence that gives me awareness on a given day. My hope is that by getting your take on something, I can gain some direction or way of looking at it I hadn't considered. And the biggest reason I access you is that I like the flow of the connection I feel. The connection reminds me that there's something beyond this temporary life. It gives me comfort to connect and know that this life isn't all there is. Knowing that you and yours are there to connect with takes the edge off the fear of being afraid to run out of time. I like to know you're there. It's like I know Mom is back at the house if I need her. I know she is there while I'm out charging ahead into who-knows-what.

Very good, Scott! You hit the mark we were looking for. You cleared some channels by digging for that understanding. It is as if we were to ask you who you are over and over in rhythmic repetition. This would push your persona to dig into its inner core. Your core would at first become defensive then it would either want to run or choose to engage in the exercise. We recommend engagement.

By engaging as you did and looking deep into your core, the understanding just popped out of you. You knew when it hit. At first our prodding caused you to become defensive and you felt, as you said, uninvited. Then you started to look inside and thought you were stuck but you kept looking and struck gold. You did not give up and once you dropped the defensiveness, the clarity hit you. That is the secret. Pose the question. Repeat it to yourself like a catch phrase over and over and start to look inside. Go to a place of center in your gut. Get out of your head and relax and know the answer will come.

Just to be tender, we are not implying you cannot engage us. We implore you to do so. It is why we are here. We know of your fears and your insecurities of physical life.

Most of us have experienced them for ourselves. You are not alone in your quest for peace and fearless existence. Everyone wants to be jeopardy-free. No one wants to keep having to look around the next tree to make sure there is not anything waiting there to eat them. The big bad wolf is just part of life. If he were not there to keep you on your toes, there would be no challenge for you to engage in physical life. The challenges are offset by the gratification of overcoming adversity and learning about what your best is.

I like a good challenge but some days I just want things to go easy.

It does not have to be hard. You have the power to make it fun.

It frustrates me when you say that. I've always thought that I was chasing some end result in life where the fun and easy part would show up. I thought that by working hard and being responsible and well-meaning, I'd find the road to riches and contentment. Things haven't really gone as I would have hoped. I'm not complaining, but I still have this sense that if I stop, something is going to get me. I can't say what that something is. It's just an innate energy that I carry that keeps me restless. It's like if I'm not moving, I'm dying.

So you are saying that there is an imaginary end zone out there somewhere that when you reach it, then you will be happy and life will be wonderful all the time.

Yes, I guess that's what my perception is. But at this point in my life, it seems that I'm just chasing my tail trying to get to that end zone.

Scott, the end zone you are looking for does not exist. It just does not.

That's discouraging to hear.

To enter the game with high expectations is the way to win. Goals and desire to achieve are the end game. You are already in the end zone, you just cannot see it. Keep the expectations out there in front of you, like dangling a carrot in front of the horse. That is what keeps you moving. Keep goals in mind and never stop wishing to achieve. You do die, in a sense, if you do not keep moving. Your body was not built to sit. It was intended to keep moving and hunting and exploring. The body mechanism is a machine that requires stimulation. As for your being happy when you reach your imagined end zone, you are going to look long and hard trying to find that. The end zones of accomplishment are many, not just one. You have many victories in everyday life that have to be viewed as end-zone arrival. You are tending to try to put all of your eggs in one basket with the view that there is nirvana waiting out there ahead of you.

For your consideration, may we suggest that you remember that life is full of purposeful ups and downs.

There is no road to the last stop where everything is permanently euphoric. There has to be the end to one adventure for the next adventure to begin. Your daily existence has to be looked at as an adventure worth exploring.

You are bound to have moments of recall where you think you are on a treadmill and you might wonder if this is all there is. The reality of the thought is yes, this is all there is. There have to be lows before you can experience the next high.

This is the game, this is life, and this is the way the cookie crumbles. So in your mind, you must find the switch that activates the outlook, "I am here right now in this place and I am having a great time in this moment." Or you can keep that switch in the off position and focus on being uncomfortable with being uncomfortable. Does any of this mentoring help you?

Yes, it does; it's just that once again, I need to process all that you have said, which I will, and hopefully incorporate into my thinking.

As I'm processing, I'm recalling a story about a woman who was in a restaurant-management training program and she was told to stand at a counter and just hand drinks to people for a full eight-hour shift. Her world for a full eight hours was a three-by-three-foot square and her reason to live was to be pleasant and hand out drinks one at a time. She related that she was determined to be the best drink-handing-out person for this shift who ever lived, even though this was not a rocket science situation. The other view she could have taken was, "I already know how to do this, so what else do you have for me to do?" I'm wondering if the difference in these two views is what you're talking about.

Indeed, Scott, your analogy fits very nicely. Taking the view of being or doing the best you can takes your focus away from the realm of being uncomfortable. It immediately moves your energy into a different space. You can walk through that portal anytime you like. It is just a matter of deciding to do it and being conscious.

How exciting! I have never gone through a portal before. Thanks for the guidance.

YOU ARE HERE TO EXPERIENCE

Scott, know that life is a series of experiences. That is what you should be tethering to your side like a string of fish you just caught. The experiences line up on a cord called intuitive self.

Experience after experience connects in your life to make you who you are now. Do not deny who you are and do not deny who others are. The encounters with other souls are gifts in your life, so to speak. Every encounter you have lines up on a cord – your life experience. You do not want to look back and say, "I did not do that." You want to look back and say, "I did this and that and, oh yes, that, too."

The source is waiting for you to return with your experiential trophies. The source says, "I will send you out, my little ones. You bring back to me your experience, no matter what it is. I will revel in your triumphs and your misses no matter what they are. I will immerse myself in the experience of your experience."

At the end, there is no mark carved in stone or flag raised in your honor to celebrate your accomplishments.

There is knowing and congratulations for showing up and there is your star that hangs in the universe. It is the star of commonality that we all share. It stands for life.

The lives you share are, in fact, the lives of one. And diversity is an important factor to consider. It is not a sin to be unlike another, assuming there even is such a thing as a sin. It takes many to make up the whole. As to who you are, be advised you are on a journey of grand proportions. There should be no regrets. Just be ready for the next adventure you choose to create. And if corrections are needed, those can be added along the way.

For now, friends, be at peace with who you are and listen for the next bell that turns your head and says, "Listen to me. I am calling you to this experience." It is a grand way to live, knowing your next experience is only a breath away. Say good-bye to your fears and nestle in the fact that you are loved and surrounded by genius and guidance. We care for you now and later, no matter what choice you make. We address the end of this session by saying once more, you are loved and surrounded with support. Do not deny who you are and be vigilant and loving to yourself and others.

DON'T FENCE ME IN

I'm recalling a photo of myself as a toddler in diapers, encircled by a portable wire fence. I was put inside this makeshift holding pen so I could be outside and not wander into the area where a tractor was digging a new septic tank hole for our house.

I do remember walking to the edge of the hole that was being dug to look inside. I also remember my mother calling to my dad, who was closer to me than she was, to grab me before I fell in. That's probably what led up to the enclosure. I don't recall the event of being in the fence area but at some point my mother told me the story of the pen. She added that I wasn't happy being caged up that way.

Basically I was crying and pulling on the fence. I don't know how long I was in the pen or if I got my way and was relocated.

My awareness of this remembrance is that it correlates to my knowing I don't like to be restricted. That's probably why I don't have an office job and am self-employed.

Scott, I have something to say about this. The fence episode says a lot about who you are as a person. You are not one to be hemmed in and it is not always easy to anticipate your next move.

You are an explorer, for sure, and you do not hesitate to take a left turn to check something out. Your knowing of yourself is spot on in that you cherish your freedom and, may we say, your tag line should be, "Don't Fence Me In."

Scott, let me add, just so you are aware, from my vantage point I see you are already clearing. Your energy is shifting. Are you not glad you are here? It was worth it, was it not, to be at this seminar?

Yes, Gabe, it was worth it, I must admit. I could whine a little and say that I'd have preferred to jump right into the book but then without all the prelude and shifting in awareness, there wouldn't have been a basis for the book. I have to say it's been a huge experience.

Scott, I think you are actually getting it. Congratulations!

A BIT OF HISTORY

It was a very cold day by my standards in Columbus, Ohio, in March of 1950. The high was 37 degrees. I arrived on the planet to take my place among those who had arrived before me. So started my existence in the physical once again. I say 'once again,' because I'm sure I've been here before on many occasions.

Being a kid in the fifties, you'd have to lump me into the group called Baby Boomers. We lived on a small farm next door to my father's parents outside a small town north east of Columbus. It was kid heaven for me, I'd say, and my grandfather was my go-to guy.

The farm wasn't what supported us. It could have been termed a gentleman's farm. My grandfather was in the insurance business until he retired and my father was a corporate type on his way up the ladder for an aerospace company. Otherwise our life was definitely rural.

The adventures seemed endless for me. There were fields to run in, sheep to deal with, six acres of woods to explore, and three fields of rotated crops to drive tractors in and ride a horse through.

Being raised in the fifties, I was exposed to Bible study and Sunday school by a very well-meaning maternal grandmother. So I cheerfully went to Sunday school, always enjoying the biblical references along with the coloring and cutting and pasting that went on around Sunday school character art work. More than once I was exposed to the stories of Moses and the other big names being spoken to by God.

The story that was always prominent with me was the one about the burning bush that talked. What I noticed was the only guys that got to talk to God were the big names of the time. You never heard any stories about Joe the peasant having direct orders from the clouds. So I guess the emphasis of the message to me was God only talks to the celebrities of the era, and how could you possibly think God would talk to you?

Even as a kid that didn't sit well with me because I don't like being left out of the game. I suffer from always being afraid I'm missing out on something, gosh darn it. So in the realm of biblical teachings, I scored low points at being okay with, "God only talks to the few."

Mr. Disney really did me in one night. I was not expecting a defining moment to show up courtesy of Walt and his Sunday night family show. The short version is I was in pajamas and a kid-sized bathrobe watching the black-and-white television in the corner of our living room. It was Sunday night prime time, the last show before bedtime. On this evening the Disney hour was talking about cats.

There was a cartoon segment describing how revered cats were in the ancient Egyptian culture. Cats were so revered that they were put in the tombs of a Pharaoh after they died. Of course, the cat was also dead. My mental kid scanner went off and somehow I got it that the Pharaoh died and the cat died and wait a minute... I'M going to die, too! That was a pretty scary realization. It haunted me for years and still has some influence over me. The realization would send me into fear-driven panic attacks that I'd have to shove down inside to preserve my sanity.

I remember dating a girl in high school, Gloria, who was very settled and comfortable with her religion. I don't know where she got her conviction about God and so on but I was still running on my Disney episode. Having her as an influence, I thought I'd try to connect with her stillness. It might be better than panic attacks. I went to church with her and her family and I always felt so not-part of the scene. I could never achieve her level of connection and serenity and belief in the process. It just wasn't settling to me. All that faith stuff was nice, but I still wanted a direct line to God. And I didn't find it hanging out with Gloria and her parents.

After high school Gloria and I went to different colleges, she to a Christian-based school and I to a mainstream college. The separation basically sent us our separate ways. I kept plugging away at my business degree and found more solace in dating and fraternity parties than I did in trying to find God. But my interest and concerns about an after-life never lapsed.

The strangest gift I remember the universe presenting me with in college was out of necessity for space reasons. At the fraternity house where I lived, I had to room with the strange duck no one else wanted to share space with. His influence sent me into some directions that opened me up to thoughts I hadn't yet generated on my own. Like bending time, for instance, and out-of-body experiences. Craig became one of those fortuitous, unexpected encounters the universe likes to dole out.

By the time my college career was ending, I met a girl I was enamored with. Let's call her Sharman because that was her name. I fell head-over-heels for this one. I spawned what I now know was an endorphin rush of epic proportions over her and, from the way she talked, I thought it was mutual towards me. The night I met Sharman, she was part of an airline crew that was over-nighting at a hotel across the street from the nightclub where I was bartending in Phoenix.

I had found the one. She was all I could think about. In the months that followed, I'd see her when she flew through on her job. We managed some time together and short stays here and there. In the months that followed, I arranged a trip to New York where she lived and I even met her parents. Her stepfather was some superhero to her and she referenced him a lot. I don't think I really sold myself to her mother. I remember her mother having very guarded energy, now that I think about it. At the time I wrote it off as 'whatever.' I still had an incredible time on this journey and assumed it would continue forever.

There seemed to be just one little glitch, however. My one forever had just converted to Catholicism and was fully immersed in that philosophy. I even considered investigating and looking into it myself for her sake and our sake as well. On one occasion we were sharing and I brought up the subject of reincarnation, time-bending, and astral travel, all of which I was exploring at the time while still looking for the burning bush to talk to.

Isn't that all normal stuff to be sharing with a Catholic convert? Let's say that after the New York trip and sharing our religious views, she started pulling the plug on our relationship. Which is easy to do when you're two thousand miles apart. I was devastated, to say the least, and didn't recover quickly from that departure. I went through the experience of, "What am I supposed to do without you?" And, "Why are you okay? I'm dying here."

Having been so immersed in this woman and then going through the emotional pain I experienced at the end, I vowed never to fall in love to that depth again.

When I look back, it's amazing in one sense where that one encounter took me; there were many gifts in that relationship. One included being exposed to the airline industry. I thought being a flight attendant looked like fun, so I applied at her national airline. I thought, "I'll show her! She isn't better than me." I didn't get the job; apparently the universe had other plans for me. So I applied at a regional airline and did get the job. For five years I winged my way over the western United States, giving oxygen demonstrations, holding up safety cards, and making customers comfortable when I wasn't spilling coffee on them.

The time off this job gave me was great. I essentially worked half a month. I did handy-man work on my days off, pursued the art of flying an airplane, and considered the possibility of piloting airliners instead of riding in the back of them. To add to the lineage of my experience with Sharman, my future wife and I met as flight attendants, which was another entire learning experience. If it weren't for Sharman, I'd have missed out on some incredible and death-defying flying adventures, endorphin rushes, and exposure to what not to expect in a relationship.

Hi, Gabe. I know you have something to share here.

Yes I do, as a matter of fact. With you being able to sense my arrival, it makes it easy for me to drop in. I want to thank you for your willingness to let me do that.

Gabe, you have it all wrong. I keep thinking that you're the one who knows what you're doing and I'm happy to step back and let you take over.

I wanted to say that you have an insatiable appetite for the dramatic. I see it in you all the time. That is a blessing, in a sense. I find you captivating in a subtle way.

Scott, it is wise of you to realize there are many offshoot paths that life can take as the result of just one encounter, the gifts of which may not be revealed until much, much later. You are blessed with awareness of the value of the potentials in any given event. As you perceived, there are untold possibilities in the simplest as well as the most by chance, bizarre, and seemingly impossible happenstances. You just have to have the awareness to be vigilant and see them.

YOU GET WHAT YOU ASK FOR

Scott, when you look in a mirror, what do you see? An image, for sure. Certainly a reflection. And it is easy to say, "This is me, I am what I see." Actually you are not what you see in the mirror. You are not as you appear to be. You are a reverse image of your true self. No matter how you comb your hair or dress yourself, you cannot see who you really are in a mirror because you are backwards. Hence, you are an anomaly. You see what you think you see, but truly you cannot see anything correctly because you actually perceive the reverse version.

You and all others tend to go through life seeing and acting on what you think you are viewing, based on your senses. But in reality what you are seeing is all backwards and distorted. If you could see through unfiltered eyes, you would see you are living in an entirely different reality than what you perceive. That is, if you saw things and actions as they actually exist, you would have to change your view of the world. However, it is not likely that you will do that. But you can become aware of who you are and how you are in relation to what is going on around you. As you participate in your life, be aware of your surroundings and the state of appearance ahead of you.

Question the teachings you receive and see if they are a fit for you. Try to see the world for what it is, not as you have been told it is. The proof in the pudding is your accountability to who you are. Make your own rules. Try to adhere to a way of life that suits you.

Gabe, I have to ask a question because I'm still not settled on your explanation of creating my own reality.

During any day, every person on the planet is exposed to hundreds of events. The events I speak of range from simple everyday tasks to unexpected and seemingly unwanted happenings, like car accidents. People's lives include pleasure trips gone wrong, steaks cooked too well done, twisted ankles, and so on. Are you suggesting that all actions by any given person on any given day have been at some level orchestrated by that individual? Aren't there any accidents or unseen, blindsided occurrences? I'm having trouble believing that there aren't any accidents or victims. I surely think that sometimes things that happen to people simply fall into the category for circle of life or just random acts. How about when someone wins the lottery? There are a lot of people trying to create that reality, yet most don't. I'm wondering if I'm about to hear you say there are no accidents. I don't know how to make all of this mesh in my mind and still fit in your teaching.

Scott, let me put to rest a couple of misunderstandings about circle of life. Yes, things including people live and die. There are the predators and the prey. It is a natural order that exists in a situation where all life is operating in a theater where no superior being is throwing the system out of balance.

There are many systems where life evolves and fends for itself on a daily basis. It is the process of life. Your life structure on this planet has evolved past the point that that kind of natural order can take place. There is a predator, of sorts, that has disrupted the order. That is man, of course.

Your presence as a human affects the systems of all things, as does every other human on the planet. If you were to take all the humans off the planet, then the law of natural order would return to its primal operation, since there would be no need for soul-related activity.

Your impact on this planet is out of control, in a sense. It is finding its own new equilibrium. So the circle of life on this planet is not the mainstay of the order. Yes, circle of life is a reality and it applies. However, the action of man has tempered the truly random acts of nature. Man's energy action on the planet alters the natural flow of events. Yes, there are accidents and there are misgivings but, for the most part, they are self-generated on some level to suit the soul progression of an individual at a life happenstance level.

If that sounds too intellectual, let me say it this way. You can experience an accident physically. And the accidents that you experience, to a degree, range from minor and annoying to life-threatening. It would be fair to say that the serious encounters with seemingly unwished for events are more likely to be self-generated ones. Events that seem catastrophic could even be a consequence that links to a previous action. Also consider that sometimes what you might perceive as an accident could be a warning in disguise or an alert from your higher energy.

But you need to know that the simple action of spilling a glass of milk can have a far reaching influence on one or more people both singularly and collectively.

OMG! I know where you got that example from! I haven't thought of that moment for years.

I did not think you were going to see that one coming. I do so enjoy catching you off guard now and then.

Scott, it would help if you would kindly share the event that the example came from. Share all levels of connection with the parties involved. The influence was profound for such a simple 'accident.'

The example that Gabe is speaking of had to do with an experience I had with my son, Austin. At the time he wasn't old enough to drive and he sometimes spent time at the house of a girl he knew and was interested in from his karate school.

This particular evening when her parents came to pick her up at the karate school, Austin was invited to their house for a short time and I could pick him up there a little later.

This girl's name was Stephanie. She and her parents were very outgoing and cordial people. When I went to pick Austin up at Stephanie's house, I was unexpectedly invited to come in and have dinner with them because they were just sitting down. I accepted and Austin and I joined all seven of them at the kitchen table.

About half way through the meal, someone knocked over a full glass of milk. As it happened, Austin and I emotionally braced for the fall out, only to witness Stephanie's mother very calmly get up and imply that the event was no big deal and started to do what needed to be done to clean up the mess. The others at the table reacted the same way. No screaming or gnashing of teeth happened and the dinner went on smoothly.

What you need to know is that as a kid at my dinner table, there would have been a lot of reactive phrases, with shame and blame thrown in as well. Austin, having a very reactive mother, was used to similar energy at home.

When he and I witnessed the calm that took place at Stephanie's dinner table, we both were struck by how different the energy was in this household compared to what he and I were used to. The point being that we were shown a different way to be. It affected us both so deeply that it was the first thing we talked about as we left Stephanie's house to go home. What a gift for him and me; it was an example of choosing another way to be and break a pattern that we had been caught up in.

So, Gabe, would it be safe to say that there's no black and white answer to my question other than yes, sometimes there are accidents and victims and sometimes there are accidents and lessons?

I think you put that well.

Here is another point to consider. You are an individual in an environment that is spinning all around you. You have chosen where to live, where to work and play. Basically the way you live, for the most part, is determined by you. Even those of you that would say you are here doing what you are doing because you have to, are in reality here because you want to be. You do not have to do anything you do not want to do. Straight up, you are free to choose your destiny, even in controlled conditions. You can refuse to participate in anything. That decision will then cause you to experience a different set of actions. There are consequences to deal with when you choose to participate and consequences to deal with when you choose not to participate. That is the grandeur of being immersed in the process of being on this planet. You cannot not play the game. The second you are born you do not just have your toe in the pond; your entire being has jumped in the pool. Do you see? You need to be very clear that you chose to be here. You chose to be you.

Scott, you are still wondering about accidents.

Yes, I am.

Accidents fall into a category of lost focus. You see, when an action you call an accident occurs, there are events that precede the actual happenstance that you might deem undesirable. There are no accidents. That might seem like a cliché to you. Having said that, understand that any action you take, even something as simple as brushing your teeth, is a result of steps taken that lead up to the actual event. Then that event which you just experienced is actually a step leading up to another event. All actions are intertwined.

Knowing that all actions are intertwined may seem inconsequential, but one action leads to another. If you are not on point with each action, then the second you drift off point, the path changes. The course alters. Good or bad? Who is to say? Simply the experience will be different than what it may have been otherwise.

Scott, you like to make things out of wood. You are always cutting wood with one of your saws. Especially your large table saw. That tool has a very large spinning blade on it. When you turn on the saw, it makes lots of noise. You pick up the wood that you are about to cut with your hand and you have to guide it with that hand past the spinning blade.

You certainly have an intended outcome for the wood after it passes the blade. You also have an intended outcome for the hand that is holding the wood. You want your hand to be intact after the wood passes the blade.

The action of cutting the wood is preceded by the actions of selecting the piece to be cut, measuring the wood, and setting the saw up to cut the right dimension. Should you be out of focus in any of these steps, the outcome of the desired end result can be different.

Note that when you are using this saw you are, for obvious reasons, totally focused on the action of guiding the wood past the spinning blade. That focus you are engaged in is called being in the moment. You are not thinking about anything else in those few seconds except keeping your hand out of the way of the blade and guiding the wood for a straight cut.

Let us say someone else walks up to you while you are cutting the wood on your saw and starts talking to you. Their action could distract you and you could lose your focus. As a result, you could be pulled out of your moment and you could make a crooked cut or lose a finger or both. You could call that an accident. You could also call it a learning experience. One possibility is that you might learn that it is better to keep your focus at all times. Or you could blame the party that started talking to you while you were using the saw. You could even get mad at the saw.

Given these possible outcomes we would prefer to have the value seen as staying in the moment and maintaining focus. The other choices of shame and blame are examples of not taking responsibility for self and accepting who you are.

Gabe, what about the person who's driving their car through an intersection on a green light and gets T-boned by another car that ran the red light? Let's say that the person with the green light gets hit in the driver's door and dies. Is this an accident or a learning experience?

This query spans more than one universal teaching. There are multiple ideologies intertwining in an event such as this. To break down all the alignments in such a scenario is a daunting task. That is not to say that it cannot be explained, because it can. However we need to first lay down a lot of groundwork to facilitate your understanding. The groundwork includes the topic of reincarnation. Suffice it to say that the event you described truly is a learning experience on many levels and would have far-reaching effects to include the person who is no longer in the physical. There is growth for all entities to be experienced in such a happening.

Gabe, I have to say here after receiving the above, I'm feeling somewhat like a deer in the headlights, reeling a little mentally. I'm wondering if what you have just given me is too out-of-the-norm to convey. I wonder if there are those that would want to burn me at the stake for sharing this thinking.

Scott, I sense your staggered reaction. You did not see this rendition coming. Continue with the receiving and see what you get. It may be too advanced for some and too elementary for many. There is also a stratum of minds that is just waiting to hear this speaking.

Okay Gabe, then let's push on.

WHO ARE YOU?

To all souls. It is your destiny to understand who you are. Primarily because you are, as are all, children of the universe. You have not been told this before. For the most part, you have been taught to believe that you were separate and not good enough in some way to be counted. You were taught that you are separated from your source and that you are not worthy enough to be in its presence. You were taught that in the event of some error, you are to be punished, maybe even physically, or banished of heart. To your credit, you have persevered in spite of all of this influence. The time has come for you to look at your existence in another way. You are invited to see that you are stellar and an integral part of the universe. You are being called upon to see the light from beyond and become aware of what part you play in this thing called 'life.'

You have not been allowed to see what is on the other side of the door of your life. You have only been led down a path of hope for the reward of salvation. Figuratively, you have been sequestered away in a darkened room where you were told about a light that you should strive to access and connect with, yet you were never given the key to open the door to this room.

And even though you have not been allowed to view what is on the other side of this entrance, at times you have seen a light shining through the cracks of this locked door.

More than once, you have queried where this light was coming from and its source. You were not told that you were worthy to have access to the key and that you could open the door.

So you are standing in front of the locked door now and you see the light shining from around the edges. We would like to hand you the key and depending on your curiosity level, you can use it to open the locked door that is in front of you, or you can put the key aside.

Gabe, what you have just given me seems rather biblical in a sense. It has a tone about it that I'm not used to being a part of. I'm more oriented to a direct tone of something like, "Get in, sit down, and hold on." Where do I go from here?

You will understand in a moment. The direction is purposeful. It is a beginning or lead-in to a concept that is being presented. You are being handed a suggested direction that is new to some and needs to be approached gently and with care.

Okay. I'll get in, sit down, and hold on.

As you evolve, you gradually come to know who you are. That is a process that takes place in many ways for many people. Finding out who you are is an ongoing experience. There are roads that lead one person to a destination that may not take another to the same place. The natural order of seeing who you are generally includes the process of emulating those around you. For the most part, even animals in the wild would flounder without the examples of their parents.

Models demonstrate to you a way that you can see. They present you with options for your consideration that help you decide who you want to be. Along with the obvious modeling, be aware that just like the image in a mirror, the models in your life are not entirely who you think they are. Be cognizant of the obvious behavior as well as the subtle influences that seep into the crevices of your being.

As you observe your models, know that you choose to emulate or reject the behavior you are raised with and guided by. All behavior you are shown may not be appropriate for you or those around you. Learn to discern and observe and then be aware of what you are choosing to imitate. At first you may choose a behavior to incorporate in your life, only to find out that it does not fit. That is key. You will know if a way of being is a fit or not by the way you feel. Try a way of being and then tune in to the rumblings or exaltations that it generates within. You will know instantly. Adoption of a particular way of being is not one-size-fits-all. You have to try on a few different coats to see which one has the best fit and feel.

Learning who you are is like looking at yourself in the mirror. You can observe yourself in dim or bright light and you can try to see yourself in the dark. You first have to decide what your motive is. Then the decision for which light you choose to see yourself in becomes easier. Clearly each level of light has its pluses and minuses. For instance you may want to view yourself in light that minimizes your perceived imperfections or you may prefer the brightest light possible so you can see everything as it truly is.

You can also try to view yourself in light that is designed to soften your appearance, as opposed to light that shows every line in your face. Sometimes you choose to use light that masks what is really there. Sometimes you open your eyes and see exactly what is in front of you. You are always adjusting the light. Are you living in the dark or do you stand in the sunlight?

We want you to know who you are. We want to support you in your process of getting to the center of what makes you 'you.' We want to wake you up before it is all over.

Most of you have not seen the real inside of who you are. Your interests may be obvious but who you are takes on a whole other meaning if you truly want to evolve. Evolution encompasses layer after layer of scrutiny and taking a hard look at the vast interior of what makes up this being of you. At times perhaps you have seen the tip of the iceberg. We invite you to explore the deepest crevices of your persona. It is an adventure like no other.

When you go down the street and see others walking along their merry ways, you should not wonder who they are. You should be focused on who you are. Do you see? The focus should be on you and what is going on in your inside and not that of others. You want to begin the process of what we call listening to your heart. When you go inside and listen to your heart, you will start to see that you are not entirely clear on the version of who you show up to be. You have not been taught to look in that direction. Your life influences have all demonstrated to you that to look outside will solve your woes. We invite you to go behind the mirror and see what is underneath the reflected image before you. And understand this does not have to be hard.

Take a moment and close your eyes and imagine an image of yourself. Create a mental room to your liking and place yourself in it. Once you have decorated your room to your taste and have put the image of you in the room, invite yourself to become comfortable in the middle of the setting you have created. Now as you see yourself in a comfortable position, visualize walking around this 'you' and note what you see and feel as you take a 360-degree trip. As you observe this version of you, ask this you what would best serve her or him in this moment. Ask what they would most like you to hear. After asking, keep the image of you in place and be still and be willing to accept what you are about to receive. You will get the answers you need. It may register with you in the form of simple knowing or mental conversation. The answer might even appear in a vision.

Your inner you knows how to communicate with you best. In this case you will be talking to yourself and answering yourself back.

I hadn't thought of going into my head to talk to myself. I have mental conversations with myself all the time. Usually my mental verbiage isn't complimentary, though. Usually what I say to myself is of a derogatory manner, where I'm berating myself for a particular action or mistake.

So you're saying to mentally see and converse with myself. You're probably suggesting that I talk to myself not in a demeaning sense, but in a positive and inquisitive way.

To step back and see yourself in a created setting changes the dynamics of how you will approach yourself. You would not talk to another person the way you speak to yourself in your mind. By creating a mental duplicate of yourself, you will be more objective and patient and less likely to attack your being. Seeing yourself as another person will allow you to more objectively see what it is you need to take the next step in your expansion.

Gabe, you now have me wondering what it would be like to encounter myself. What if I don't like me?

We find that an amusing thought. From our perspective, there is nothing about you not to like. That is not to say there is not room for expansion in terms of your outlook. There is always the next step and sometimes when you look back at a way you used to be, you wonder how you thought and acted the way you did. But remember at that previous moment, you were the most advanced, enlightened being that you knew how to be.

You need to know that the you that you will encounter is the you that you are going to be. If you look at this new encounter as a meeting of a mentor, it changes the energy of the meeting. It's very difficult to not like the new improved you. You really do not have anything to worry about.

So find you in your mind, appreciate who you are, and learn from the you that you are evolving to be. This could be remarkable.

WOULD YOU LIKE CHOCOLATE OR VANILLA?

Scott, let us present some thought processes for you to consider.

"This whole thing is your doing." "You have only yourself to blame." "It is all your fault."

Interesting phrases, would you not say? To read or hear any of these phrases generally would bring up feelings of defensiveness. To have another person look at you and utter these or similar phrases could likely cause you to either strike back in some way or run away, depending on your fortitude.

Pick a situation you can remember when you were full of shame and blame toward another person. What if you were to view that remembrance from a different vantage point?

What if you changed your recalled version to include the thought, "I created that experience," or "I made that event happen to include the awareness of 'There is a gift in any situation.'" If you can view that past event with different eyes, the energy surrounding that whole experience shifts.

Initially, you might resist seeing an unpleasant past event as something you decided to have happen to yourself. "It is just crazy to think that I caused that to happen to me. Especially when it was clearly their fault." Or you could likely be saying to yourself, "I did not create that event. I was just minding my own business." This is an understandable reaction, especially when most likely all of your models are exemplifying the same outlook.

In the course of an average day, the events in one's life could cause one to say, "The life I have now is not one that I would choose." You might say, "How can you tell me that I would choose a life of difficulty and strife? How could you tell me that one who is suffering great pain would choose that in a planetary experience?" You might also express, "There is no reason I would choose a life that is full of struggle and obstacles. For instance, why would I choose a life where I was a refugee in a war zone? Why would I put myself in such a situation of existence?"

The answer is, there is no reason to do such a thing unless you wanted to experience the situation at hand. To help the seed we are planting here, let us give you an example. If you were a person in a third-world country, you could view that experience from different points of view. You could see your life as, "I am a poor victim of my circumstances and I am doomed to a life of strife just to survive." Or you could have an outlook of appreciation for having what you have at any given moment. These are extreme states of minds to have, for sure, but they illustrate the range of thought processes one can choose to participate in.

If one were to write a book, the paper before them initially is blank. The possible sequence of words that can be put on that paper would be endless. Your life is much like the blank sheet of paper is to an author. The choices of actions before you are endless, yet most choose a series of safe, reserved actions to participate in.

Ask anyone, "What would your book be about? Would it be fantasy, fiction, or an expression of real-life experience?" In any sense on some level, it would generate feelings of the heart. Maybe it would be about what moves you to tears or moves you to joy. It is different for everyone. Each person chooses to react differently to different situations. There is no rule that says you have to act a certain way. And there is no rule that says you have to write your book on a certain topic. You get to choose the topic, much like you get to choose which way you turn when you walk out your front door. Do you see?

Your life needs to be viewed the same way. You came here to write the pages of your life and find out what moves you to tears and what moves you to joy. You did not choose to participate in the mundane.

You have unknowingly succumbed to social stigma that appears to say, "You can only behave this way." That philosophy may apply to some systems but not socially.

Social structure dictates how group energy should intermingle for the good of the whole. Our suggestion is to be a rebel. You get more bang for your buck!
Speak of your experience here, Scott.

Okay. I wasn't expecting to be called on. Give me a moment while I scan my memory banks.

Scott, speak of the train drawing.

I'm still scanning. Oh, do you mean the drawing in Sunday school?

Yes, precisely. That is the one. It is a perfect example of how you as children are encouraged to conform. Relate it clearly and concisely.

I had forgotten about that. Okay, Gabe, I'm dialed in. I'm remembering that it was a Sunday school class that I had never been to before. I probably was dropped off there by my maternal grandmother on one of my Sunday outings with her. There were a lot of other kids in the class and I didn't know any of them. All the tables were full and there were kids seated on either side of me and across from me at my table. Once we were all in place, we were each handed a printed 8x10 paper with a black- and-white picture of an old-time steam locomotive. There was a box of well-worn crayons in the center of the table for us to use to color the train.

I was surprised because the woman in charge told all of us, with strong energy in her voice, to wait to start coloring the train; then her instructions followed. We were asked what color the train should be and eventually the kid consensus was the color should be black. So we could only color the train black. That was the word from on high.

For some reason I didn't like that I could only color the train black. I was being corralled, fenced-in, and limited in my self-expression. I resisted the instruction, even though I knew that every locomotive I had ever seen was black. So I chose an orange crayon and proceeded to create the first orange locomotive the world had ever seen.

The little girl seated to my right noted my departure from the instructions and felt it was her duty to report my rebellious act to the attention of the lady in charge of the kid room. I was amazed at how quickly the teacher reacted to the informant and came my way to verify the information.

The teacher very enthusiastically informed me that I hadn't followed the instructions to color the train black. She made sure the entire Sunday school room was aware of my deviation. Being chagrined at the unexpected attention and scolding, I said, "I can fix it," and proceeded to try to color over the orange with a black crayon. I don't remember the rest of the morning in that class but I'm thinking it would have been more evolved on the part of the teacher to have recognized me as a free thinker or a man who marches to the beat of a different drum. Instead I was exposed as a not-following-the-rules type. In this instance I could have been a positive example for the others to see. There just wasn't any thought given to putting that view in place. Of course, all of that adulation wouldn't have helped the hierarchy's need to keep order.

Gabe, is that what you had in mind? That's all I can recall of the event.

Your story perfectly illustrates what we are trying to convey. You went to a place of nonconformity, which is a strong suit for you, and were made an example of for others

138

to criticize. It is a time-tested scenario that through the ages has been used endlessly on many levels. The manipulation process that the teacher was using was intended to limit dissension in the ranks, as it were. "I will shame you and I want the rest of you to see this and know the same thing can happen to you." You were little and vulnerable to the programming. And some of the programming is still in place to this day. You are inclined to follow the crowd until you are not. You have become more of your own person in recent years, however.

As a side note, be aware that the teacher's actions had been modeled to her somewhere by someone previously in her life. In that moment, she was doing the best she knew.

Certainly, she could have acted differently toward your free spirit, but that option did not exist in her tool-box at that point. She was using the only tool she knew to use.

Our encouragement for you is, do not be afraid to be a rebel. Look at things differently than you normally would. Look behind the scenes and do not just accept the frontal view. Take side roads and see what you have not been shown before.

In the process of finding the rebel within, you have to be cognizant of what you have been shown by your models. Along your road of life, you have been taught that rebels are looked down upon and eccentrics appear abnormal. Yet each has its place in the whole. We would encourage you to be the light-hearted rebel. If you are offered a choice of chocolate or vanilla, say, "What the heck, I will try both!"

Salute your status and be dramatic and attract attention. That is what you came here for. You were looking for adventure when you signed on the dotted line. Being a happy rebel is an excellent way to experience on a grand level.

Part of living as a happy rebel is choosing an optimal viewpoint of, "I created this experience." Note that this outlook shifts the responsibility, of course, to you. That may be a hard concept to grasp. It is much easier to point a finger in the other direction, rather than turning that hand and finger at yourself. But that is what has to eventually happen in the process of expansion to help you see who you are.

So in the course of life, be the rebel who chooses the different approach and cast your models' influence aside. Try your own concepts on for size and see what serves you. What serves you also serves others you are near.

Section IV

**It's not what happens to you,
but how you react to it that matters.**

Epictetus

WHY DID I CHOOSE THIS TO HAPPEN TO ME?

Gabe, as you present these latest concepts, I start to mentally create examples of very unpleasant situations and experiences that I'm sure no one would want to participate in.

They are necessary, you know.

Gabe, why would a car accident or a broken leg or a tumor be necessary?

In fact, here is a real-life situation I personally encountered recently. An acquaintance of the past named Betty recently found me after 16 years to get some plumbing work done for a small remodeling project. On the day I worked for her, I was finishing up as she arrived back at the house from work and we ran into each other at the front door.

There was the obvious exchange of pleasantries, and then our conversation quickly turned to a condition with her left leg. She had developed cancer in her knee and was receiving radiation to treat it. She was wearing shorts so clothing wouldn't rub on the blistered area. The area around her knee looked burned and damaged from the treatments and she could still walk but it wasn't easy. The drama of the story was that she'd had some surgery to deal with her knee condition some months earlier. In the first surgery something wasn't done correctly. This malfunction then caused her to need additional procedures that she otherwise might not have had. One of the additional issues was the current radiation treatment and pain she had to endure from it.

So basically Betty felt that the first doctor messed up her original surgery and now things were a bigger mess. She started to cry as she was telling me about all of her knee treatments gone wrong and then she started to share her fears of, "What if I can't work or I end up in a wheel chair and I might lose my job because I'm missing so much work and the doctors are going to have to graft skin to my knee from my back?" and so on.

Betty is a strong, independent woman and, not having seen her in 16 years, I was surprised that she felt comfortable enough to use me as a sounding board. I hadn't anticipated this encounter and was, of course, sad for her and feeling helpless because there was absolutely nothing I could do to help her except just stand there and listen. I empathized to the best of my ability and let her open up.

Finally I could see Betty change her emotional course and pull herself back up to her strong side, so I continued to listen as she reentered her focus – life would go on. As she regained her composure and went inside to get off her feet, I wrapped up what I was doing.

So Gabe, I'm having trouble seeing where Betty would have created this experience in her world for any reason. And did I create that encounter with her for some reason in my existence? Just how far does this creation thing go? Is there something I'm missing here?

Yes, you are missing a big piece of the puzzle. Now do not beat yourself up as a result of us having said that.

The act of creating is far-reaching, most certainly. Few are aware just how far life experiences reach beyond the obvious initial interaction.

Betty is going through what you would call a tough time in her world. We know and can see that you felt helpless in your encounter with her. You were there for more reasons than to do the plumbing her house required. She was not expecting to open up to you with the turmoil of her leg. It was unanticipated on her part.

You loosened her up with your attempts to bring her to her optimistic side. You were a catalyst for her energy to realign. By saying what you did, you freed her from some pent-up fears. She was able to lean on you in a way that cleared some of her channels. She is unaware of her situation, other than the obvious physical malady at hand. She does not realize she chose the issue. She is unaware that the universe is knocking on her door trying to get her attention. You can see this, but she cannot. Nothing you could have said during your encounter would have made any difference to her because she was upset and consumed with her own fears.

Your heart felt heavy that you could not help in this situation. That is your nature. You did your best by just being quiet and letting her expose her feelings and fears. That did her the most good in the moment. Do you see?

Well, yes and no, Gabe. My bottom-line question is if she did in fact create this thing with her knee, how did she do that and why would she manufacture this malady? First I want to know so I don't self-inflict some misery on myself. Second I really want to know why she would create that experience for any reason. In my world we're supposed to have fun. And to me, she didn't look like she was having fun on any level with her leg thing. So in this moment I'm willing to go along with the teaching that the issue with her knee is part of her experience. But why?

First, let us say that you are wise to know that. Your life has taught you well, or should we say you have gathered much of what life was setting before you.

In her case, Betty is surrounding herself with painful memories of life and ways of being that have not suited her. Wrong decisions, if you want to use the word 'wrong,' plague her from an internal place. It would be more accurate to say she has chosen to dwell on past events in an internal sense and apply deep regret emotionally to those happenings. She is constantly ridiculing herself on an internal level that generates energy conducive to such a malady.

The mental process that would serve her would be an attitude of, "Oops, that did not work," or "Oh, silly me; I will try it a different way next time." Instead she is using a mental process of self-condemnation.

The energy that surrounds such thinking is like boiler heating water. If the heating energy being put into the tank is left unchecked, the water gets too hot and expands to the point that the boiler will eventually split, buckle, or erupt. It is just a natural happening of cause and effect. Too much energy put into too small a vessel will in time have to express itself somehow some way. In the case of the boiler, it is an explosion; in the case of a body, it is cancer that occurs. In Betty's case the heat being put into her boiler is the negative thinking she generates toward herself. That energy has built up inside her body and is trying to find a release point. Instead of having a boiler that will split, buckle, or erupt, you have a human vessel that generates maladies of the flesh. It is that simple.

To further fuel the concept here, there is a gift for you and Betty in this situation.

Gabe, hearing you say that sort of hits my resistance button. What could possibly be the gift for anyone in having a radiated knee?

It depends on how you look at Betty's situation. Which, by the way, would serve both of you to do. Betty could lie back on the couch with her leg elevated and her wrist dramatically poised across her forehead wondering, "Why me? Woe is me for being a victim of cancer." Or she could select the thought process of, "What is there for me to learn from this situation that would better improve my outlook on things? Maybe my life is trying to tell me something."

There is a substantial difference in the two different outlooks, Scott. Do you see?

Granted, I see that clearly, Gabe. There's a huge difference. I'm just wondering, given the same situation, if I'd have the awareness to make that switch in my thinking. And I'm wondering if I could pull off that mindset conversion. Would it be too much to remedy, too late in the game, sort of thing?

It is never too late. Remember that. Learn now or learn later. The universe does not care when you get the essence of the teaching. It is driven to make sure you get educated, no matter how long it takes.

The remedy for you and all others is to adopt the shift in your thinking now before you need it. However, if you can make the shift now, you will not need it later. This kind of thinking is easier to create when there is no pressure, as it were. Betty is fully capable of shifting in an instant even now, but she has a lot of distractions to deal with at this moment in time that make the shift more monumental to achieve. Let Betty be your model and let her be a gift to you and all that you share this example with. Take the turn in the road now before you hit the barricade at the construction area. Simply put, choose a different road before this one takes you to the bridge that is out.

A shift in the thinking process on her part would serve her and her health. It is never too late to produce a different thought. Shifting to the, "What can I learn here?" approach moves the energy of the situation to positive. It adds a degreaser to the wash water and starts to dissolve old stains. Energetically, things will start to happen for the better, which directly affects the physical on all levels. It takes the negative energy out of the boiler. If you turn the heat down or turn the fire off, the boiler is under less stress. Eliminate the stress on your human boiler. Turn down the negative thinking, and the boiler is in a better position to carry on. Do you see?

There are untold gifts waiting for Betty to claim if she wants to see them. Note the universe has upped its game here, trying to get Betty's attention. There have been shots across the bow that Betty has chosen to ignore in the past. The universe is not tapping on her shoulder now. It is hitting her over the head with a club in the form of her knee situation.

That might be a stretch to understand, but she came here to learn and has gotten off track and the universe is screaming to her that she has taken a wrong turn and should course-correct. The crisis at hand will cause Betty to have new awareness and change her outlook. It sometimes takes a crisis to make you see who you are.

You can hang around at the bus stop, waiting for the next thought-provoked crisis to arrive, or you can take action and start looking at the way you are thinking now and alter your course while you can.

There is an Italian word that we would like to insert here and that is, "Capiche?" Our understanding is that the use of that word means, "Do you understand?"

Gabe, I'm not one to hang around waiting on anything. I tend to go after something rather than waiting for it to arrive. I'm totally intrigued by what you're presenting, however you said that all energy interaction is very far-reaching. So how far is far?

Far is far. That is for sure. The levels of depth cannot be calculated.

Energetically, the influence of human interaction travels through millennia. The process is so subtle that any thought you have about another traverses the universe. The effect you have on another is a grand adventure for both parties. You are never done with the other, once you engage. The energy put in play in any encounter is ongoing forever.

The ramifications are obvious. You enter data from your thinking process into the universal data bank. That draws the attention of the universe. You could liken it to your internet system and search engine monitoring. The more traffic you generate with your thinking, the more it aligns you with others in the same category, whether you want to be aligned or not. The grouping you receive on the internet is a direct correlation of your input. The universe will group you the same way. Energetic positive thinking gets aligned with similar activity. Negative resistant thinking has its rewards as well. Like attracts like.

So again, Scott, it is an energetic choice. Do you want to align yourself with those going to the carnival or do you want to walk around with an attached ball and chain. Just like choosing chocolate or vanilla. You have a choice. Neither is better in the eyes of the universe. It will support you in your chosen direction.

Okay, Gabe, I think I'm getting it and I don't mean to appear to be resisting you, but I'm still struggling with some of this.

Recently, there was a terrorist attack in another country that killed approximately 30 people in a train station. From any perspective I can muster, there were 30 innocent victims. These were people just going about their lives and… bang! The party was over because, in my view, some misguided soul wanted to have the experience of setting off a bomb in a crowd of people.

Was any of that an accident? Were 30 people on some level wanting to create the experience of being blown up? That's just hard for me to get my head around and apply what you have previously presented.

As we proceed, Scott, we would like you to pause for a moment. Center and relax. Your energy is all disrupted from your expression in the last paragraph. You need to listen to your heart in this moment. You are very passionate about trying to understand why such things could happen to good people. Your caring energy is highly aroused. We wish to comfort you with some gentle thinking.

Your caring side certainly does not want to see 30 people suffer such an event. It upsets you when you see seemingly unnecessary tragedies occur. Your caring side knows there is another way. We want to explore this occurrence more with you if you wish.

I do want to understand the process of such things.

Scott, in the scenario you have presented, there was danger presented to many. Few were spared from the attack. There were those who clearly suffered more than others. There was pain and trauma experienced by many that will be lived far into the future. No doubt, no one would want to knowingly experience such an event. Here we must reach deep into your core and take you into a different perspective that few knowingly go to. The perspective is from a high vantage point looking down. Much like one would see from an aircraft.

As you look down from the aircraft window you see before you a landscape. You most likely will not see all the interaction of human forms taking place. Your bird's-eye view does not show you detail, but you know there is interaction taking place. You know, for instance, that there is lightning striking the ground someplace. You know that there are children being born and that houses are on fire somewhere. You cannot prevent any of the events in play. All you can do is center yourself in your world at any given moment and see who you are, without suffering another's pain which is not your calling. Your calling is to understand who you are at any given moment and help others to understand who they are.

You are not in a position to be able to understand why on a given day, 30 seemingly selected people placed themselves in an experience with shattering results. What you cannot know are the purposes behind the lives and events of that day. Some of the deaths were purposeful, in that the death of one might have the result of inspiring another left behind. One's death might be a gift for another left living. The universe does not respond to anything but focused energy and the energy of the 30 people who died was cohesive enough to generate the end result. Each of the 30 involved had a soul mission that you are not aware of. Much like you really do not know at times what your soul mission is for you.

Gabe, I have to take a break from this recent information because it seems like we're going down a rabbit hole. Is there some simple laymen's terms you can use to explain why 30 people chose the experience of dying in a terrorist attack? The reason I'm not letting go of this is because once I get out in the world, someone is going to ask me a similar question and I'd like to have an answer for them.

Scott, the simple answer is because they wanted to.

Gabe, I'd have to say that probably isn't the simple answer I was hoping for.

We said that to get your attention. You have not been able to understand until now the true meaning of creating your own experience. The depth of explanation is not truly relevant to this narrative. Suffice it to say that they chose their place and time to transition for a myriad of reasons. Let us present some understanding that will clarify this.

When we said that 30 people wanted to experience a terrorist attack, it would be more accurate to say that their SOULS wanted to experience a terrorist attack. Let us use your experience of Kathryn as an example.

Gabe, do you mean Kathryn that I met through my son's friend?

Yes, that Kathryn. Speak of her agreement with her husband. That is a perfect example of choreographed soul level experience.

Okay, I hadn't thought of that. Good idea you just had here. Thank you. I guess that's why I keep you around.

Okay. To start, my youngest son Heath had a friend in high school who knew that I was a plumber and essentially referred me to his mother. So through our kids Kathryn and I connected and set up a time for me to come to her house. On the day I arrived, I tended to the plumbing issue she was having and then we got into a conversation about our sons.

As we talked, I found out that she was a math teacher by trade. She was also a single parent and had another son who was older than my son's friend. Kathryn had been widowed when her kids were young. It was surprising to me because she didn't seem old enough to me to be a widow. I had assumed Kathryn was divorced. So she was a mom doing her best to do what moms do and deal with the rigors of single parenting, including her youngest son's chronic asthma.

In the course of conversation, her way of speaking got my attention because it reflected someone who was comfortable connecting with the other side. So I threw out the subject and discovered she did light channeling. That got my attention and was basically the connection point for her and me. Over the course of time that I knew Kathryn, I'd call her on occasion get her take on things that were rolling around in my head.

As time went on, I got to know Kathryn through some sessions with her and, of course, there was our sons' friendship. One day, she told me how her husband had died unexpectedly. I don't know how the subject came up, but she went on to say that she had been mad at him for dying and leaving her alone to raise the kids. I found that a little amusing.

The more she spoke of her anger, the more intrigued I became by her story. Being intuitive at some point in her development, Kathryn did the climbing through the veil thing, found her husband, and did a lot of venting. When she was finished with him, he got his turn. The gist of the response she got back from him was to be reminded that his early death is what they had agreed on and to get over herself. It had been their plan from the get-go, before they came to the physical, that among the norms of life, they would come here, have kids, and he would leave early.

At the time, that was an OMG moment for me. Because first, that such a plan seemed so casual! Second, that you're planning an Earthly journey together? And you actually coordinate your departures, referencing events, and life processes? From this side, I wonder how that could be so matter-of-fact. How could you sit there with another and say, "Okay, this is our plan. I'll help you get things started and leave early; you finish the party and clean up the dishes. Does that sound like a plan? Okay, good, let's do that."?

My wondering is how different the view must be from the other side, as opposed to what it looks like from here on Earth while one is in the middle of the ball game. When you're planning your strategy, you're relaxed and not thinking about the actual blood that might be spilled on the playing field. Is it really that easy to sit on the other side and be so matter-of-fact about setting up an entire life scenario? How does a soul not be codependent about anyone's role in the performance? It would imply that there's not a lot of meaning attached to the trip. It sounds like it's a trip to go slumming with the physicals.

So, seriously, Gabe, we plan this stuff just to see what happens? I'm not sure where to go with that one.

Scott, the situation described by Kathryn is a perfect example of two souls aligning themselves to create situations that will cause learning to grow at a soul level. Such planning is not necessarily at a level where you plan simply to have a lark. There is deep consideration involved between souls that head out to connect in given situations through the vehicle of physical life.

Their planning session was like two people discussing what to wear to a costume party and being very serious about it. There is rich intention put into such encounters. Think about all the effort, trials, and tribulations that an entity goes through in the physical to reach those calculated encounter points. In the planning stages entrance into physical does not appear overly complicated and there are great intentions set in place.

The departure from the heavens is not taken lightly or casually, Scott. To choose physical life is not for the faint of heart. It takes courage to decide to get on the playing field. And it always seems like the game will be a lot easier before you jump into the action.

The example of Kathryn's pre-incarnation meeting could not be more simply and clearly portrayed. It is a simple yet very deep illustration of how the universe and souls orchestrate scenarios to indelibly etch experience for teaching purposes. Do we have your attention?

You have not been able to understand until now the true meaning of creating your own experience. The depth of explanation is not truly relevant to this narrative. Suffice it to say that the 30 chose their place and time to transition for a myriad of reasons. There is no better proving ground to test one's soul expansion than the physical. You jump in the ring and test your skills to see if you have trained correctly and note where you can improve on your trip to the top. Through physical experience, one can find the weak spots in their beingness.

Kathryn's soul had a definite plan and so did her husband's. You would have to talk to their souls to know what those plans were. When you encounter seemingly tragic events, you have to fall back to a perspective of what the soul is seeing, not what your physical eyes are registering. There is a difference in perspective, just like an adult might view a situation differently than a child would.

From the soul perspective, the plan to come, have kids, and one of them leave early is a straightforward everyday occurrence. Much like a couple planning an outing for the day. For the most part the planning is oriented to anticipated experience. The family attends the outing knowing that one of them needs to leave early and they plan accordingly. Everyone comes home at the end of the day with new experiences logged into their being. The soul side, however, has much more clarity and vision of intent as to the purpose and needs of the excursion. Once in the physical, a person is not as pragmatic, loses their clarity, and is more likely to experience confusion related to seemingly unexpected, although actually planned, events.

In Kathryn's case, she was having fun at the park and did not want the party to end. Her husband loved her enough to depart early to allow her to go down the slide at the park and learn a perspective in life that she could not have learned otherwise. Take the example of a child that seemingly departs too soon. Given the soul perspective, the departure could be viewed as an interactive gift setting up a situation of deeper growth for those who remain. What an amazing gift!

Souls that sometimes seem to tragically depart early are simply souls who willingly took part in a play. Their gift to the other cast members was to take on a small interactive part that would heavily influence the other actors' deeper roles as the play continues. Does that perspective help you, Scott?

Yes, it gives me a view that anchors me somewhat. At the same time, it takes my breath away. It's a perspective that in the everyday world I never hear anyone sitting around talking about or teaching.

Yet Gabe, even with your last examples, I'm a little confused here. On one hand you have said that we create our own realities, and then on the other you have illustrated that we have a life plan in place before we get here. That would imply that anyone's life at any given time is set in stone, so how can we create if everything is already in place? It seems like two opposing views. Which one do I focus on?

Scott, the answer is both. You do come to the physical with a plan. But you know as well as anyone that nothing goes according to design. Your initial plan is a road map, of sorts. Your life can turn on a dime and you can haphazardly be involved in a life interaction you had not planned on, which could modify the previously planned life lesson. So the plan gets altered somewhat. But keep in mind that the overall soul goal generally stays intact. Sometimes you take a different route to the store, but you still get there and bring home the groceries.

You can go on automatic pilot and just let life take you where it will and the plan you came in with will more or less take place. HOWEVER, and that is a big 'however,' you can remove the blinders and push life to the limits. You can choose to sit in your easy chair or you can get up and question things. We recommend the process of querying the universe and seeking to be led to new understandings. It is the difference of choosing a life that takes you through all the basic levels of education one at a time in sequence, versus being the person that is so hungry for information that you skip a grade because you learned ahead of time what was at the next level.

When you live a life thirsting to find out who you are, you throw off your original schedule of departure. The timing in your life changes, the universe accommodates itinerary changes, and maybe you decide you do not need to go to the train station and depart with the other 29. It can happen that originally intended courses are altered. Do you see?

So, Gabe, you're saying that even though I came in with a life plan as such, that I can alter that plan once I'm here?

Yes, Scott, you alter the plan a little each day. And some days you return to the original plan. There is a lot of winging it going on while following a general, pre-planned route. Your chosen life sequence is like having a planned vacation and then, on a whim, taking an unexpected side trip to parts unknown. If you are tuned into taking advantage of an unexpected event in your life, you could alter your entire expansion process and cause yourself to expand sooner than expected. If you get the lesson sooner than planned, that is okay. Then your itinerary gets changed and you do not make a stop along the way that you had originally expected. The universe will change the ticket at no charge. In fact, it encourages you to make extra stops as often as you can. The universe wants you to really, really, really enjoy your trip.

Let us return to your question and concerns about the 30. There may have even been 40 at the original meeting. They simply had a much larger planning party than Kathryn and her husband.

The purpose of the party was to assist them in their immediate influence, as well as you. Yes, you. Look at the event in which those 30 souls participated. It has even affected you and your soul learning. There was even a gift from them to YOU. The event of the 30 caused you to look inside a little deeper than you would have if the incident had not occurred. Imagine that. That perspective takes the game to a whole new level, does it not? Your soul has expanded a little more by their decision to participate in the event at the train station. Maybe you were even at their planning meeting. In their trip down the slide, they learned and expanded and so did you. What a gift!

Also, on another level, consider that the 30 were thinking like one, but simply took advantage of a common event. On the singular level, each was leading a life independent of one another. Your friend, Betty, was thinking like one. Her singular thinking process produced her current *physical discomfort. The 30 took it to a higher level and created 30 individual experiences that came together in one event. They did not consciously sit down and have weekly planning missions to pull off the event, but their combined energies got the attention of the universe. The universe simply responded.*

Scott, it would certainly seem calculatingly cold to say that such an event was created by the universe, but it is truly the process that took place. It is a very simple and powerful process. Now we would like to take this subject back to a singular level.

Understand, Scott, that there is truly caring energy that exists in the universe. It cares so much that it will allow you to experience whatever you desire. It will even protect you along the route until you go through your desired event.

As you think, so the universe responds. Its response is imminent and powerful and the energy that you put out in your thinking process is registered, measured, correlated, cross-referenced, and acted upon. So be mindful of how you think. Your thinking process is what causes the trip to go forward, backward, or sideways. That is one more facet we would like to see you understand here. It may not be what you want to hear but it is what you need to hear.

So Gabe, I'm guessing if I asked about the six million people who died in concentration camps in World War II, you'd give me the same answer – the universe responded to people's desires. That was just the next example I had on my list.

There were many interacting energies that created that event. There were innocent souls swept up in that event, for sure. There were many participants at many levels that formed the thinking that materialized that event. It was not brought about overnight. It was the culmination of many lives generating much energy over many lifetimes that manifested such a global occurrence. It all goes back to the process of energy being generated by one or millions. It just took a long time to overheat that boiler. But it did overheat and the energy was released in the form of global conflict. This is a highly philosophical subject and we are not intending to dissuade you from your current belief structure.

Our material is intended to supplement your idea of who you are and give you some pause to possibly create change in how you look at your life and others as they live around you. You will evolve and grow, no matter what roads you choose in life. Possibly with some new understanding so the roads ahead will have fewer potholes.

Gabe, as I dodge the potholes in my road, do you mind if I present another singular situation that has my attention?

It serves us to serve you on any question you have. There are no unimportant questions. That is how you learn. We will always answer your queries. Go ahead, my son.

A SHORT DEVIATION

Gabe, this is completely off the subject that I'll return to in a moment. I'm slightly startled when you refer to me as, 'my son,' and I've noted that you sometimes use the term 'we,' and sometimes you say 'I,' when you're referring to your energy. It's not a big deal to me; it's just that I notice the variation in the responses.

Scott, when we use the term 'we,' we are applying group consensus to answer you. When you hear the term 'I,' it is coming more directly from me as an individual source. On the other hand, to call you 'son' is a term of endearment. As we work with you energetically, you fit the role of the inquisitive child looking for answers and we relish that experience. It brings out the parent in us all. There is no need to feel slighted with us using one term or another. It is all intended to come across as affectionate and supportive.

That is the way I take it, Gabe. It was just a noticing on my part. Thank you. I do so enjoy the connection.

BACK TO BUSINESS

Okay, Gabe the question I started to ask you was about a man I met on a job some time ago. He was a middle-aged man and the repair I did was under his kitchen sink. It was the type of repair that caused me to need to hang around for a while to make sure the repair was going to stay fixed. I didn't want to have to go back.

So while I was waiting to make sure it held, he and I started to talk and this is when I heard he had been experiencing a lifelong heart condition. He told me his heart was enlarged and also related the ups and downs he had been through physically. He shared with me some of his crazy treatments, including battery packs as a power source to jump-start his heart and so on.

I'm wondering about all you have explained and I'm trying to correlate this man's lifelong condition with how he created it. If he truly created this malfunction of his heart, when did he have the time to do it? And on top of it all, he seemed very accepting of his condition and was very grateful for each day that he woke up.

Scott, you have done it again. You have opened another door! Let us look inside and see what we find. Open it slowly, as there is a lot to maneuver around in the room you are about to enter.

Your question is related to the concept of reincarnation. Having mentioned reincarnation, understand that there are life adventures laid out to meet the soul requesting the experience. Any soul about to reenter may lay out a course that will take them through a series of events or expose them to circumstances that will facilitate learning on a level that can be experienced no other way.

This gentleman you met was yet another gift to you because he allowed you to learn more about who you are and are not. He chose a life of physical challenge to develop just the outlook that you mentioned.

In a sense, he was testing himself against previously learned principles and he wanted to see if he passed the test. He has reached his attitude of gratefulness by living the life he described with you. He would not have had that understanding ingrained in him had he chosen another life of say, more normalcy. Do you see?

His current life experience facilitated his development of gratitude for life in general. A more healthy body would not have supported him as well in the goal. It was a soul desire to have the experience of deep gratitude for the gift of life.

163

His heart condition has been a tool, of sorts, to enhance the chance to learn to have this outlook that you witnessed. He chose it. You and your soul would perhaps choose another way to ingrain the same lesson.

Gabe, your having said that sent my brain to being a young boy and how more than once, other boys would single me out, in a bullying sense. It was like I had a sign on my forehead that said, "Go ahead, pick on me." For the most part I would just be minding my own business and the testosterone would be thrown my way. I don't know why I drew that attention or whether it was a male rite of passage. I didn't see it happening to other guys. At least not to where I noticed it. Of course I learned from it and became more cautious about picking my battles and deciding when to run, among other things. Would you say that I created all those aggressive encounters? I can't see what the purpose for that would have been.

Scott, all encounters of any sort are intended to create learning. Even if you attempt to not learn, you are still given the opportunity to learn. In your case, you learned to discern your enemy, but more importantly you learned to stand your ground and take different tactics. You learned to access others differently and defuse things before discord took place.

Your crowning victory was the evening in college where you and your date were approached by the two gentlemen in the park. Do you recall? You two were outside taking a break from the gathering that you were attending.

I had completely forgotten about that, Gabe. Yes, that's what happened and they were up to no good. I sensed we were about to experience an unpleasant situation and wasn't sure what was going to happen next. There were two of them and just me and my date.

You played it well. You went to the action of inviting them to the party nearby and acted like you were not concerned by their presence. You presented energy as if they were old buddies to the point of starting to walk to the building and insisting that they come along. That defused their intent. They were not expecting your reaction and it befuddled them. That was very shrewd on your part. It saved you great consternation.

It was an event that would have gone differently if you had not had the previous aggressive encounters as a young boy. Those experiences taught you to think differently. One of your soul's goals in this life has been to learn not to be afraid. You chose those scenarios to help you learn and test your skills as you evolve.

You are still testing yourself as an adult. Only now it is not the aggressive adolescent who is getting in your face; it is the tax man or the trials of running your business or the once-in-a-while unreasonably demanding customer. Those events you chose served you. Just so you are aware, we were at your side. You did not know, it but we were there, my son.

Sorry, Gabe. I have to pause here. I don't mean to interrupt the flow of what you were giving me, but your having said you were there at my side brought up a lot of emotion for me that I have to process.

Part of what ran through my head was I always feel alone, no matter what I do. I didn't know you were there but I'm grateful. So were you around more than just on those occasions that I was being hassled?

Scott, we were never more than a whisper away.

We are pleased to say that you have kept us on our toes. You have not been lackluster in your activity on the planet. You have made our job interesting. It has to this point been a delight to have been at your side. We can only be excited to see what you are going to bring to the table next.

As to your feeling alone, do not despair. There can be the tendency to feel alone in a crowd, especially if you are a way-shower. Because you are always out ahead of the crowd exploring the next path, it creates a situation where you are alone because you are in the lead.

I hadn't looked at it that way, Gabe.

Connection is more energetic than physical. You are tuned to be alone more often than not. Your way is to listen and stand back so you can see all. The experience for you is showing others the way to proceed, having been there yourself. You revel in guiding and helping others to see what you have seen. That is your connection point. That is part of who you are. Be okay with that. We are here to connect whenever you need to plug in.

We want to be clear that you must understand who you are. It is necessary for you to see the true self that you have to offer to the world. You will be understood and heard and welcomed with open arms. There is yet another great adventure for you out there. We will be at your side and continue to see you through your chosen venue of precarious inquiries. We love you and adore your tenacity to proceed.

Gabe, I have to ask. Why would you love me so much? Of course, I'm flattered and I thank you but what is the motivation for you to be so engaged? Why would you love so much the energy of 'Scott'? What's in it for you? I mean that with curious affection.

I have my limits with the people around me. When I see people give up on themselves and don't want to come along for the ride, I just have to say, "Okay, see you later, have a nice life." I don't have an agenda for another's outcome. I only know to present some options and let them choose and proceed on their own. I'm not one to beat a dead horse, so I just push on. How do you maintain such a constant ongoing interest in being at my side? I don't see myself as that interesting.

It is easy for us to maintain the interest you speak of because, my son, you do not give up on yourself.

Scott, you are not one to stop in your tracks and turn off. For the most part when you are in a tight spot, you do whatever you can to wiggle out of it. If the way out is not immediately clear, you adjust your mind to the situation to try to make it a win for all involved.

Gabe, I guess that I'm fortunate that you find me so amusing. Does every human have a support group such as yourselves? Can every human turn around and see an energetic entourage in their wake?

Scott, it is an interesting question you pose. You are attuned to understandings that most are not interested in.

The short answer is yes! Anyone who wants an entourage gets one. Suffice it to say that all humans have energy support. If one is inquisitive and wants to experience the connection, the universe gently complies.

We are servants who engage in spiritual support, if you do not mind us using the term 'spiritual.' There are multiple realities at play here if you really want to go down the path of what is. Suffice it to say that to truly describe our existence in minute detail would be difficult for you to comprehend on a functional level. It is all energetic. And you have the luxury of connection with it at any time.

You could call us 'angels' or you could call us 'Joe and Associates.' Even calling us 'Susan's Team Members' could apply. It is important to see that any vernacular you want to attach to us and are comfortable with will work. You can call us whatever and we will answer. No matter what tag line you attach to us, the call still comes through to the correct extension.

As to our dedication, you have to know that is what we do. We derive our essence from our connection to being part of all that is. To guide and assist is our hot button, if you must know. Our perception of you and your activity is not like you would think. We do not see you as a reality show playing over a long course. We see you as an entity exploring your environment looking for new possibilities. We see you much like a young child reaching for new things on the next higher counter.

As a child grows, it reaches heights that allow it to see what it could not see before. As it grows a little more, it can reach items on the counter that it could not see or know were there before. The curio on the night stand or coffee table that could not be seen weeks before is now within reach. You live the same way conceptually. You grow a little and then you can reach the next thought that you did not know was there.

As you engage in your passions in your existence, so do we in ours. Our passion is watching you grow.

Knowing that you're watching is making me a little self-conscious. Maybe I shouldn't run around in my underwear.

There is no need for you to be ill at ease. We are energetically merged in a way that you do not perceive. We see you but we do not, if that makes any sense to you. Your day-to-day movements are not monitored. There is no security camera in place watching your every move. So be who you are and frolic when you feel the need for that expression. Your moments are all yours. That is, unless you seek us out, then we connect on a different level. So go amongst your experiences and feel safe from our viewing or judgment, because you are.

Okay, Gabe, one last thought on my part here. I'm one of 8 billion people on the planet. If all humans choose to have a cheering section such as you and your energy, how is there enough of you to go around?

If you attempt to calculate as to how many of you there are and how many of us there are, the numbers would not compute out. You must know that from where we sit and where you thrive, there are different theaters of operations. There are different systems in place that operate independently of each other, but still use the same energy. To explore the process would be impractical. The deep questions you ask are akin to how many angels can sit on the head of a pin. The answer is it does not matter. Just know they and we are here. That is said not to scold you, but to keep you centered in your awareness of here and now. Do you understand, Scott?

I think so. That answer will hold me for now. What the heck, I can always ask you the question again after I grow a little.

Section V

Work out your own salvation.
Do not depend on others.

Buddha

WHERE WERE YOU ON THE
DAY OF THE ROBBERY?

Gabe, I have a friend, Gail, that I've known for years, as a result of having common ties to mentors of the past. Once in a while she calls me for small plumbing issues that I help her with. When I do have an occasion to see her, we catch up on what's been going on and I fix a leak or two. And then say goodbye until the next encounter.

At our last meeting, Gail was very energized about an event that she had been through and was anxious to share the story. She has a deep belief around the existence of angels and their protective qualities for self and settings. The premise is that you call in the angelic help to watch over you and your environment. And there are the archangels that you can ask for guidance as well as protection. This is a strong belief for Gail.

She is very active in this practice on all levels. The teachings of the angel concept were something Gail and I had been exposed to at the same time. Gail took the concept to heart more deeply than I did. I don't dispel the practice; I just don't embrace it as much as she does.

With that background it's easy to understand the energy she had in telling me her house had been broken into in broad daylight while she was at work. She had left the house in the morning, set her angelic protection button, and went about her day.

When she got home, a front window had been removed over her kitchen sink and both of her bedrooms had been ransacked. Of course she felt violated and was surprised that her two dogs didn't deter the intruder.

Her losses for the most part amounted to a lot of costume jewelry that she was sentimentally attached to. She had been saving for a new computer, had cash placed in corners of her house for the purchase and was happy the intruder didn't find any of that.

The point of the story for Gail was the fact that whoever the culprit was got past all the angelic protection in place. What the heck! Were the angels on a break?

I have to admit she got me thinking about spiritually requesting protection and prayer, etc. I could relate to her frustration in a way. I found her experience puzzling for me in a philosophical sense. I want to believe that there's energetic help to call on in times of need. Naturally she was upset with the belief versus the unexpected outcome. I found her story interesting and baffling at the same time.

Of course, Scott. Her story is interesting but it goes back to – she created it.

She would have difficulty seeing where she was the one who brought the occurrence into her life. However, when all is said and done, she has gained wisdom and value from this experience that she could not gather any other way.

Scott, from our vantage point it looks like Gail's angels were right on task. Maybe they should be given a badge of courage. Maybe even a raise. Her angels did not shirk their responsibility. In fact they went to great length to protect her from harm.

Please note that there was a subtle process going on here. There was an event or an orchestration of sort taking place in Gail's life. Note that there was no bodily harm to her or her animals.

Next note that it was during the day when she was gone, so she was not endangered. There was no destruction to her property other than the window removal and the intruder did not even break the glass. He could have just banged his way in.

Then notice nothing of real value was lost save for the sentimental value Gail had for her costume jewelry. She did not even lose any of the savings for her new computer.

There was a message for Gail here that she would not hear any other way. Her angels took pretty darned good care of her, actually. They did protect her and her possessions.

Gabe, do I dare ask you if you can tell me what the message was for Gail? I have a feeling that I know what it was but I'm thinking you could be more accurate in the answer.

You are guessing that, you know. You do not and cannot really know. The message for Gail is loud and clear if she is willing to grasp it. The message is not always what it seems. Her soul is on a mission of experience and expression as is yours. Take for instance your goal to know no fear. Her soul goal is not the same.

Her growth is in the area of attachment to personal items. She knows no limits to possessions. You surmised that might be the area of concern her angels are dealing with. But in reality you cannot know what her soul has in store for her learning. Just as she would not really know what your soul has in store for you to learn.

There were gifts for her in this experience and she would be well served to walk away from the event with the recognition of what the true gift or awakening is for her in this happening. That is where the growth on a personal level is. Growth means awakening to a new understanding about old ways of looking at things. Sometimes it takes a shock to make someone look in the mirror. When the lesson is learned, the soul relaxes a little and lets out a sigh of relief and goes, "Ahhhhh." The soul then looks over at the angels and says, "Good job, you guys. Now get back to work. Let us get to the next lesson."

Gabe, I'm always amazed at how many different ways you can show me how to look at a given situation. I enjoy that. Now let's get back to work.

IN SEARCH OF THE BURNING BUSH

As you know, one story I carried with me from my Sunday-school days was the tale of the burning bush. That bush that talked to only one guy on one occasion. So where do these bushes grow? I want one for my backyard because it would be a good type of plant to have here in Arizona. It probably wouldn't even need much water.

As a kid being exposed to the biblical world, my thinking was if God would talk to someone, why not me? I still wonder about that. I don't separate myself from the powers that be. I want to do interviews with them. I just figured no one's been brave enough to ask. So I decided to ask the first chance I got. I set my sights on stepping out of the box.

I've always derived comfort from and was drawn to what I'd call stories of connection. I'd say that being talked to by a burning bush was a pretty big deal. It doesn't get much more exciting than that. Booming voices, fire, smoke, and so on. You know, guy stuff. So you can see why I was attracted to that scenario. Since they didn't have phones back then, maybe burning bushes were the only way to go.

Being curious by nature I decided to set my very young persona in search of a way to talk to God and have Him answer back. What got my attention once was an encounter, I'm telling you, that I had with Jesus. That's correct, just little ol' Average Joe, me. I was maybe 6 or 7 at the time, standing near the front of our house. The door was open and I could see the stone driveway that ran through our big country yards. Our front yards bordered pastures and were separated by a fence and tree line. I could see the trees along the fence line swaying in the wind that day, as I looked through the front door from inside the house.

I was headed outside from the kitchen through the dining room to the front door. I remember something sounding in my head that was not me. I call it 'voices without sound.' To me it's like having a thought go off in your mind that you know isn't your thought.

That was the first time I'd had this experience, so I froze in my tracks. I clearly knew it was Jesus. I knew all about him from Sunday school. He was talking to me and I didn't question it. I just wondered what was going on. I categorically heard him say in my head, "Scott, I'm with you all the time."

The wonder of it all, to me, was the receptive process. I'd never had anyone or anything jump in my head before. Being all of 6 or 7 at the time and having Sunday school under my belt, I went, "Okay," and ran outside to play. You know, it was just another day. The powers that be were calling from the heavens. There was nothing out of the ordinary about that.

Just to qualify the above experience, I'm fully aware that my upbringing had me oriented to God and Jesus. If I had been raised in Asia or Sudan, my programming would have been oriented and influenced by other philosophies. Other philosophies, of course, revolve around other deities and their associates. In a different place, I could've been contacted by Allah or Buddha. Who knows? I say that simply because I'm convinced that whatever the divine energy consists of, all 8 billion of us who are here now and those coming behind us are dealing with the same forces. Depending on where we come from, we simply call the divine and its participants by different names. I don't think the divine crowd really cares. It's all comes out in the wash for them, I think.

Between first grade and high school, the only thing that I can say qualified as putting me a little closer to the talking bush was the television show The Twilight Zone. I loved the twists and turns of the series. It was out-of-the-box stuff for me. But I never got connected with God watching that show.

In my high-school years, I remember hearing about a happening at one of my brother's friend's house. I don't know how it happened but in some manner my brother, while at this friend's house, was alone in a room where there was a rocking chair. I have no detail of the setting, but my brother witnessed this chair start rocking on its own. Needless to say, he didn't stay in the room very much longer. This experience rattled him. My brother's fright was evident when he was telling me the story the next day. It was clear to me at this point that he and I were going to take different spiritual paths in life. He went to a place of, "It was the work of the devil" and I went one hundred and eighty degrees the other way. I wanted to have seen it happen and I wanted to know what was going on. To me, his experience was like running into a celebrity at the airport. "What were they like? Were they as tall in person as they look on TV? Did you get their autograph?" I was still looking for the dial tone to the heavens and this was as close as I had come since the first whisper from Jesus.

When my curiosity gets piqued, my way is to jump into things that I'm interested in and just see what happens. My 'fake' daughter (I don't like the term step daughter) recently saw me doing some task related to a new cat that adopted us. Unbeknownst to me, she was watching me do whatever it was in caring for the cat and she said, "Scott, you always look like you know what you're doing whether you do or not." I realize I've always carried that energy and I suppose I radiate it in my pursuit of a way to talk to God. If someone were to tell me God was in the cornfield over there, I'd double-time it, head right to the middle of the field, and disappear into the rows. No questions asked. There would be no hesitation on my part at all

Since I hadn't found the cornfield God was in, the next best thing to check out was the obvious route of religion. But to me the process of trying to find God the way religion was suggesting always left me flat. My experience of the religion process was like trying to find Big Foot. There were always tell-tail signs, but no one could ever find the guy. My other take on religion is there's a lot of sales work promoting hope. It's like being sold a new car, but you aren't allowed to drive it. You're only allowed to know it's in the garage and maybe someday you can drive it. But for now, just know it's there.

Now and then I think of a line I heard in a song – "I swear there ain't no heaven and I pray there ain't no hell." Shoot, I want to know what the real deal is. Let's stop messing around here and find out what's really going on. I want to see the car, I want to get in the car, and I want to drive the car.

I always wondered about those who were telling me about heaven and so on. How did they know if they hadn't been there? It's not like they had home movies to show me.

I wanted to be the guy taking the movie to bring back and show everyone else. Yeah, put me in coach, I can do it. I wanted to be on the playing field. Remember I wanted to ride in the sleigh behind all the flying reindeer.

I don't know why but I never was comfortable with, "If you're good you'll go to heaven." So you're saying if I mess up just once, the party is over? That doesn't resonate to me if the big guy is all wonderful and kind.

Okay then, there's forgiveness, but only if you accept the deity into your heart and maybe throw in a little praise. I was uncomfortable with the deal about praising, also. If a deity was as great as I was being told, I'd think that this deity would have his or her act together. Wouldn't a being of that magnitude be okay with who they were? I can't imagine that they would need to be told on an ongoing basis how wonderful they were.

My rebellious side still wrestles with the practice of praying. I'm not saying I don't do it. To pray is to set intention, in a sense. But to pray and HOPE that I'm heard? To me, it's like raising your hand in class and not being recognized, while another student gets called on. "Ahem, excuse me, I want some attention and I want it now. I'm in trouble here. Hello?" Maybe you have had other experiences, but praying to me has always seemed what being in space might be like. It's REALLY quiet. The sound doesn't travel.

When I was growing up, I never had anyone ever tell me I could access the big guy. You were only told that you aren't worthy. I think we all got sold a bill of goods. Being the rebel I am, I thought, "I wonder if I could put a call in to the top." So I just kept doing my thing of just jumping in whatever I was philosophically exposed to, even though I didn't know what I was doing. I gave myself permission.

I had no trouble with the idea of being equal to God, even though I knew I had some further training to finish. I never thought that I should cower and beg for forgiveness. So far it's working for me. Understand though, I haven't given up being honored and humbled by the experience of connection with the higher energies. Even though I don't know what I'm doing, I just keep reaching for the top.

I think people have to give themselves permission slips to engage with whomever or whatever. Once that takes place, everything else seems to fall in line. I play a little game when I can, as I'm out in the world. If I'm in a store getting parts or things I need for work, I'll walk up to the counter and when asked if I can be helped, I say, "Yes, I need the smartest guy or girl that you have here." Or I say something like, "I need an expert." It's amazing what usually transpires on the other side of the counter. Nine times out of ten I hear something like, "You don't want to talk to me." Or some other verbiage that implies that this person isn't the right person for the job. Rarely do I hear, "You're in luck, I'm that guy," or "You couldn't have better timing; today you got the best one here and now."

Most of us haven't given ourselves permission to be great. We seem to wait around for something outside of us to say we're allowed. Once you give yourself permission to be considered great and equal to the best, suddenly you are. You can get the scent and jump right in. It doesn't matter whether it's communicating with the higher powers or some Earthly objective. So many of us don't say, "You know what? I'm worthy. I want to do this or that and I can. I may not do it perfectly the first time but I'll get better as the game goes on and I'm going to have fun doing it." For one thing, I don't want to be beaten back. I don't want to be told I can't do something.

Based on my own experience, my thinking is we can go right to the top if we want to. And the big names will answer back. There doesn't need to be a middle man. You don't have to waste your time looking to find the potato that looks like a deity or the dairy cow with spots shaped like a cathedral.

If you get still and centered and are sincere, you can ask any question of the universe and in a millisecond you get an answer. Sometimes I get the answer as I'm asking the question.

To connect to the universe, here is all I do. I get quiet and mentally ask the question in my mind. In the beginning I'd literally close my eyes and mentally throw out my question. I'd pause, listen, and go back to what I was doing. After a time, I actually started to receive. The hard part was knowing if I was answering my own question or if I was receiving from outside myself. The more I did it, the more I could differentiate the messages. Also, the more I did it, I found I didn't need to have my eyes closed. I could just continue with what I was doing, pause a second, get the answer.

I've found that I get a lot of answers when I'm stopped at a traffic light. Anytime I'm asking in a car, of course my eyes are open, which is pretty important when sitting in traffic. Asking while doing something is effective because tasking is a left-brain activity, keeping it busy so you can bring your right brain into play. Any activity that you do that's occupying your left brain frees up your right brain to make the connection with the universe.

You have to understand I've been doing this a while, but that's the basic process. It's like anything else; just stick with it and you'll get the feel for your own method. We all have a right-brain receiver.

I was watching a talent show lately and there was this guy who was obsessed with swallowing swords and other long metal objects. I was struck that he had counted how many times he had attempted to swallow a sword before he actually did it. It was 1,336 times before he pulled it off. He actually had an exact number of tries. Passion knows no bounds, I guess. If a guy can swallow a sword after 1,336 tries, it should be really easy by comparison to learn to tune into and receive from the universe. My point is that if you send out a question to the universe as many times as this guy tried to swallow a sword, you'll get results. Just an FYI, I haven't gotten any feedback to date on the winning lottery numbers.

You can derive emotion-filled, experiential, and heartwarming connection with the top gun of your choice. I've had that experience in many ways and places and it's very reassuring to make that connection. It's way more fun to make personal contact with the powers that be than try to communicate with a bush that's on fire. Besides, it can't be much fun for the bush.

I offer this story that might explain how the burning bush was perceived by another.

My oldest son was 10 years old at the time. I had taken him and his brother to Sedona one morning for a little outing near the airport there. We had some time and I had no plan. I just thought I'd plant some philosophical seeds about energy and vortexes and see what would happen.

Sedona is famous for its energy vortexes and there's one located at the north end of the airport. On the way up to the airport, there's a pull-off to the side of the road where you can park your car and then easily hike up over some rocks and drop into the area of the energy vortex. We pulled over, got out of the car, and started up the staggered ledges to the top of the rock formation that crested up and ahead of us. As we started up, my oldest son exuberantly said, "Dad look, there are Indians up there." He was pointing straight ahead and up. I realized what was happening and encouraged him. I asked him how many he saw and he replied, "Two." I asked him to tell me what they were doing and he said they were waving at him. He was visually locked onto them; I could tell he was seeing two Indians. I wasn't seeing anything. According to my son, they were motioning us to continue on, so what the heck. We went on.

On this path from the road, you tend to go up, then you hit the high point, and then the path drops back down to some large flat ledges. You can see all of southern Sedona and Oak Creek from this point. We were just looking around at the site and my son went off again. I turned around because he was behind me. Now according to him, there was an Indian standing in front of him. I couldn't see this one, either. No problem. I knew he could and that was all that mattered. I asked him where the Indian was standing and he pointed to a spot about three feet away. My son was acting shy and coy as he pointed to the Indian's location. You have to understand that shy and coy aren't his

183

normal mode of operation, so I knew he was experiencing something out of the ordinary.

This was his experience and I wanted him to get the most out of it. I didn't negate anything he was describing to me. He was looking up at something taller than he was and then he would look back at me and then back at his visitor. I asked him to tell me a little about what the Indian looked like and he did. Then I told him to walk closer to the Indian and hold out his hand. Which he did. For some reason I knew he was about to connect with this entity's energy. So I said, "Let the Indian touch your hand." My son sheepishly held out his hand with palm up and then the Indian laid his hand on my son's hand. I could tell by my son's reactions that all this was going on.

As he and the spirit Indian connected, he looked embarrassed. He dropped his head a little and lifted his shoulders and looked at me, like, "What do I do?" I asked him to concentrate on what the Indian's hand felt like. He said it felt warm. When he said that I knew his powers to be were working overtime with him. I was so jealous. I wanted to see and be touched by the Indians, too. I didn't let any of that come through, though. I didn't want to detract from my son's experience here in the vortex.

The handshake was the high point of the encounter between the Indian and my son. I don't remember how it ended, but it didn't last much past that. Wow. I was dazed and amazed at the whole thing, while my son just seemed to take it in stride.

And as if that wasn't enough, a little while later after my son's Indian departed, we walked a little farther east on one of the ledges and one more time, I heard, "DAD!" I saw my oldest stopped in his tracks with this look on his face of OMG! From where I was standing, he was looking at an open area on the ledge. It was as if you were to see someone looking at nothing in the middle of an empty parking lot, acting like they are seeing something that isn't there. That's just what was going on.

My son was looking up and down like one would do looking for something on a set of shelves. He was seeing a log cabin that, from his description to me, would have been something a trapper would have lived in 150 years ago. I saw him back up and he was looking up, using his hands to imply size. I asked him to describe to me what was there. He went through the door of his perceived cabin and could tell me what was on the inside. He could see the roof and the windows and the door and antlers hanging on the walls, etc. He was in total disbelief at the vision he was having even as he was describing it to me. Was he having a wild day or what? I had been visiting vortexes for years and never had an encounter like that. It was an amazing event for me to witness. I was grateful and excited not only to have been there for my son's experience but also to have been part of it, for the opportunity to see through different eyes and consider different philosophical possibilities.

So where am I going with all of this? If my son could have had these visions in this day and age at the age of 10, who's to say that the universe didn't communicate to Moses the same way? Only in the case of Moses, his vision was a bush that was on fire instead of a trapper's cabin. The whole experience my son had was also a gift for me. Thanks, universe.

Scott, you never tire of spirit contact.

No, Gabe, I don't. I was just getting excited all over again writing about my son's experience.

*It is good that you enjoy spirit encounters. Where would
we be without you?*

VOICES IN MY HEAD AND GHOSTS, OH MY!

I mentioned previously that in my early 20's, I landed a job as a
flight attendant at a regional airline. It was an amazing opportunity for
me. Things took off for me there on a lot of levels. No pun intended.

Being a male flight attendant in my early 20's, I worked mostly
with women and met my wife there. I became exposed to airplanes and
got interested in learning to fly. And I actually got some hip tips about
the location of that elusive, fiery, talking bush.

At the airline, I'd work with the same crew members over the
course of a month. Then the following month schedules would change
and I'd experience four new personalities for the next 30 days. With
that grouping of people in the crews, you could get to know a lot about
each other because we spent plenty of time together on the flights and
in the airports.

In this manner I met the sisters. They were of Indian-American
decent and very vocal conversationally. They were much into contact
with the other side. Come to find out, they knew how to use an Ouija
board, and they were almost brazen about the subject, the way they
spoke about it.

"OMG!!! Seriously you can do that?" I thought. When I heard of
their skill and adventures, I had to contain myself. I figured I had just
hit gold. Maybe they'd met the burning bush or one of its off-spring.
Maybe they could talk to angels or past celebrities. Of course I wanted
to do that. I wanted to jump in and swim with the dolphins, too!

They told me how they would speak to their cousin who died in a car accident at the age of 23. They mentioned the entity they called The Captain who would come over the board. And there were others.

This was just too good to be true. I had to see what it was all about. Maybe I should see if my brother would be interested. To me, communicating with the dead goes right along with the empty rocking chair rocking by itself.

I arranged a night to meet with the sisters at their house for a session on the board. I was SO excited. I just knew this was going to be great!

On the appointed night, I arrived to find two normally-dressed young women in a normal condo setting. They had lights and furniture like everyone else and nothing was floating around the room. There were no signs of there being any out-of-the-norm ceremonial paraphernalia or altars. There were only signs of average, everyday living.

I was disappointed. I had thought there was going to be... ah, something unusual, not normal. "It's okay, Scott. Just relax and go with the flow," I told myself.

The few of us who were there got settled in chairs, with the sisters on the floor. They had turned on some music because their deceased cousin liked the music. Who knew? They sat next to each other facing the board in front of them. They were sitting so that one of them could put her left hand on the card while the other could put her right hand on it. The card was a tear-drop shaped pointer that would maneuver around and point to letters and numbers printed on the board. The presumption is the energy involved causes the card to slide around the board and point to the necessary letters and numbers to spell out words and thus reveal mystical messages.

I took a front-row seat in front of the sisters because I wanted to see everything. I didn't know how any of this worked. No incantations or flamboyant ceremonies were used. They just put their hands on the card together and it started to slide back and forth and around like one would move an iron over a wrinkled shirt. The motion was very fluid.

I noted that the pointer didn't stop on particular letters or numbers; it just kept gently weaving back and forth with the sisters' hands following the card around. On occasion, in answer to a question, the card would slide to either of the upper corners of the board where the words 'yes' and 'no' were printed.

I was totally focused on watching the sisters. The lights in the room didn't flicker. Their faces were not contorted, their eyes were not rolled up, and their heads were not rotating in 360-degree turns. They just let their hands follow with the card as it maneuvered, seemingly on its own.

They would ask a question and verbally translate the answer, rather than wait for the card to slow down and point to the letters one at a time.

Wait a minute! How were they doing that? I thought you had to wait for the pointer to pick a letter and sequentially spell out a word. How did the sisters know what the answers were? They clearly weren't waiting for letters to show up. Their deceased cousin came through and they talked to him like he was in the room. When I say he 'came through,' I don't mean he materialized; they just kept their focus and watched the card continue to slide on the board as they conversed with him. They'd interpret his words and vocalize for the rest of us in the room, and then they'd respond on their own. It was effortless on their part. I noted that there was even some joking around with some of the answers. There were no responses of hell-fire and damnation. It was just energetic connection taking place between two physical people and I don't know how many non-physical people. You know, just like at the coffee shop.

I was awestruck. I noticed as the girls communicated with different energies, the card would move with different rhythms. That is, the card would slide differently on the playing board. It appeared that each entity had its own signature with the girls, like people have different rhythms as they speak and walk. It was easy to see. For instance, the card moved around faster when they talked to their cousin than when they were talking to their friend The Captain. To me this was all freaking amazing. I felt right at home with what I was seeing and at the same time a little left out because I wanted to be able to do what the sisters were doing. Especially now that I knew what it was supposed to look like. This was one of my send-me-in-coach moments. Where do I go to get certified in this inter-stellar communication thing?

To further sink the hook in for me, at one point the girls were connecting with a message that came through from a source new to both of them. "I am a student on a journey just like you," was the opening phrase and unexpectedly, one of the sisters looked at me and said, "This message is for you." Needless to say, whoever it was certainly had my attention.

This new encounter came across as an older male, like a grandfather type, which engaged me like a magnet. That was definitely a hot button for me. The basis of the message was introductory in nature. Of course I asked a lot of who, what, and where questions. The name I was given to identify with was 'Simon.' I felt I had run into a celebrity at the airport. Simon was very non-committal about specifics and was very patient with my inquisitiveness. And through the process, the girls just kept the card moving at the pace Simon was setting and continued to interpret until our meeting ended.

Wow! There was someone or something in a land far, far away that knew who I was. How could you not get crazy excited about that? At the end of the evening, I thanked my hosts profusely and went home wide-eyed and in a mental state of high alert.

I had found my new religion. I probably was feeling like a person who's been saved and thinks they should now go save everyone else. Rather than buy a commercially made Ouija board, I made one out of wood and stick-on letters. My homemade receiver was my new 'bible.' I'd try to get anyone I could to do it with me. I wanted to do Ouija the way young girls like to text. Interestingly enough, my wife at the time was good at working the board. She never really wanted to play at it, but would do it reluctantly. She could get the messages clearly as they came across the board. I was jealous at first, but I got over myself and learned from her as we did it.

It's interesting what you learn when you're feeling obsessed and trying to save humankind.

There aren't a lot of takers. There are a lot of polite, "Okay, that's nice," and there are a lot of questioning looks. Trying to save the lot of humankind is like being in network marketing and trying to get people to sign up. It's a numbers game.

In the beginning stages of playing the board, I started to realize that I could hear the answer to a given question in my head. I'd hear the silent voice that I knew was not my own. I'd mentally receive a message in its entirety with complete knowing, rather than waiting for the pointer to stop at individual letters on the board.

Oh, that's what's going on. I get it now! The magic wasn't in the board; the magic was in the sisters. They had simply learned how to tune into whatever there is to tune into with their minds. The board was a focal point that put them in an altered, receptive state of mind. Of course that explains the sweeping motion of the card and how they knew what a given message was without the pointer stopping at each individual letter. Oh my gosh, that means we're all receivers if we just want to learn how to do it! That also means that you could communicate with the universe using a pizza box with letters drawn on it. I'm wondering, does that mean my pizza is holy — or haunted?

Another gift from my flight-attendant days was meeting and working with a woman who got me interested in a soon-to-be mentor. This mentor was a proponent of self-help through self-hypnosis. Another facet of his teaching was showing people that everyone is psychic. A lot of his seminars were oriented to this and they were always large and filled to capacity. Once I found him, I was at any seminar that he put on. And they were right up the road in mystical Sedona, Arizona.

Through these seminars, I found out I was more intuitive than I thought. This average flight attendant was finding out he could receive messages! This meant a lot of personal growth taking place for me, as I evolved my ability to connect and receive.

At one of my first psychic seminars in Sedona, I had an experience that in a sense blew me and another participant out of the water. It was the morning of the second day of the event. I'd had a strange dream the night before and just wrote it off to the weirdness of being excited about the weekend.

On that morning I woke up clearly remembering the dream, the participants, and even the names of the people involved. And the dream was indelibly etched in my mind, in that it stayed with me. It didn't disintegrate as I fully came awake, like most of my dreams do.

When I got to the event room, I took an aisle seat about two-thirds of the way back from the front of the room on the left. Others were coming in and getting settled and a woman came in my row and sat down. The energy was high in the room and I greeted her as she was taking her seat. We were talking and then there was a pause in the conversation between us. I noticed a lot of people still going up and down the main aisle on my other side. I happened to look up at a passerby in the aisle in time to see the name tag on a young woman walking toward me.

The funny thing was, I noticed the name on her tag was the same name as the one that had come up in my weird dream the night before. After she passed, I commented about that to the woman sitting next to me. I went on to tell her about the dream and as I finished she said, "Oh, you should tell her about your dream."

I responded with a questioning tone and my row-mate iterated her sense that I should share the dream with the woman whose name was in my dream. So I decided I'd try.

Later in the day, there was a lunch break and the session was long enough that there was time for participants to hang around the pool and enjoy the warm weather. So I went outside where a lot of the participants were gathered. I walked past the shallow end of the pool only to see the girl with the dream name standing waist-deep in the water, just leaning against the edge of the pool deck. She had a cigarette in one hand and her arms were resting on top of the edge of the pool.

I stopped and introduced myself and went into why I was addressing her. I mentioned that I'd had a dream the night before and that her name was in it and I just thought I'd share that. I didn't know if it would mean anything to her or not.

Of course, she was open to the share. I proceeded to tell her that what I had seen in my dream were a woman wearing glasses named Jean and a man named Bob who were worried about her and wanted to know if she was all right. I no sooner finished my story than she started visibly trembling. It wasn't a subtle little shake as if she was cold; she was trembling with strong reaction. I'd say her response was more like she had just been told that she had unexpectedly lost a loved one. I was somewhat dumbfounded to see her response to my little story.

After the initial jolt, she was obviously processing what I had told her and didn't say much to me, but got out of the pool and left.

Another lady who had seen the whole exchange between us pulled me aside and proceeded to give me some feedback on what she had seen happen.

It turned out that this onlooker knew the girl I was speaking with and she went on to tell me that only 10 minutes before I shared my dream with her friend, another participant had told her friend the very same thing. It turned out that Jean and Bob of my dream were the names of the girl's parents, including my physical descriptions of them. They'd died in a car accident and were wanting to connect with their daughter to make sure she was all right. Wow! I got to be part of all of that.

Sharing my dream with the girl in the pool likely was more than she had planned on from a psychic seminar, and it was amazing to me. Who knew I'd come to an intuitive-based weekend and actually be intuitive? The whole situation with the dream and the sharing, along with the confirmation, left me with a 'wow' feeling, starry-eyed and bewildered.

Home run, baby. I wanted to do that some more!

HOW TO HAVE FUN AT A FUNERAL

With the help of experiences at the Sedona seminars and other venues, I learned I could connect with those who have passed. I have done it a few times where I go to a service and talk to the dearly departed. I can usually pick them out in the room. I have noted the deceased might be clowning around sitting on the casket and waving their arms, sheepishly standing in a corner, or hanging out in the back of the room. It must be strange to walk into a room and be conscious of who you are and see lots of people you know and realize that no one knows to what extent you're there. Imagine being invisible at your own going-away party.

I don't think funerals really are for the deceased. I think it's a process of closure for those of us still here. I try to take the position of being happy for the departed because their tour of duty is done. Good for them. The rest of us are still slugging it out or having our way with the world, depending on how you want to view the experience.

Not being one to enjoy the emotions of grief and loss, I try to stay neutral and on the occasion when a funeral is in my experience, I just go with it and sort of practice my craft.

I had the occasion to go to the funeral of a very successful customer of mine who took his own life in his late thirties. Apparently when he was young, his father had died in a not-so-fun way from a genetic disease. Because of this, my customer never had children so that he wouldn't pass on the gene. Apparently Mark had started to display the same symptoms as his father. Having vowed not to go through what he saw his dad go through, he became proactive one day and ended it all in the back yard while his wife was out of the house.

I was struck by all of this and at the heavily attended funeral, I found him in the back of the church and touched base with him. He was his usual, quiet, withdrawn self. During his life he had influenced many others philosophically and financially. With so many in attendance, the emotions were high and there were many teary moments for all. I found myself being moved and emotional at times. And I was just his plumber.

For some reason, the connection I made with him this day was not as solid as I have experienced on other occasions. The upshot of what I received from him was that he regretted doing what he had done. He was not happy with the action he had taken. I'm guessing that kind of feeling would have to be expected when you see how many individuals' lives you have been part of. It's easy to not be aware of how many others we touch.

When I go looking for those who have left, my objective is to connect and see if they are oriented and know where they are. I try to help minimize the shock that some go through, let them know they aren't alone and that someone can see them. On occasion for the more bewildered people that have encountered, I've learned to call in help from their side to assist. If they are dazed about where they are, heaven-sent tour guides can help smooth out the transition.

It turned out that Mark didn't want help or at least not my help; he was sort of closed off in his own space there.

Next I have to speak of Robin. I met her in some local personal-development classes and worked with her on several occasions. Robin had encountered some bouts with breast cancer, which ultimately was the cause of her passing. At the point she knew she was about done, she set herself to the task of planning her funeral. This occurred over the course of about a year. Her funeral went off without a hitch. Had you known Robin, you'd have recognized her hand in the entire service. The music and the sayings that were read were all based on her outlook as I knew her.

At some point after the funeral, I accessed Robin just to check in. I surprised her when I showed up, but she adjusted quickly. She simply wasn't expecting me. The fun thing was she looked great, had a lot of energy, and was so tickled that her funeral went the way she planned it. When I first connected and she knew who I was, she threw her arms up and said , "I did it!" It was reassuring and fun for me to have such a clear experience with her in that way.

Learning to do what I can do, I found out I don't need to go to funerals except to support those left behind. I just tune in and go find the departed and pop in on them. It saves gasoline.

I have to tell you about Lydia. My connection with her on the other side was one of my best and incredibly rewarding for me. The rewarding part was that the connection was amazingly clear and through communicating with her, I got answers to some long-standing questions of my own.

Lydia was actually an aunt of my then-wife, whose family was large. Lydia was the oldest of 9. My wife's mother was the second oldest. The family was Spanish and they had ties to agriculture and ranching. Lydia and her husband had a unique ranch in eastern Arizona, which was the center of a family reunion once a year.

Over the course of my marriage I, of course, encountered Lydia. She was strong and driven and had a heart of gold. She would do things like gather up unwanted clothing and take it to Mexico to help out those who could use it. She was also a very 'get it done my way' person. She had strong opinions and could definitely be a force to be reckoned with.

The sad part was as she got near the end of her life, she developed severe dementia. The last time I saw her, she had become lost, frail, and fragile. She had come to the point where she was in a wheel chair. This was a woman who would drive a 4-wheel vehicle over terrain that a mule would think twice about maneuvering through. Her deterioration was a tough thing for me to see and deal with.

The reason I was so drawn to Lydia is because after my divorce, out of all the family I had been a part of for 23 years, she was the only one who reached out to check in and reassure me. At the time I was touched and heart-felt at her unsolicited expression of kindness and acknowledgement.

That's the reason I wanted to connect after she passed; I felt drawn to thank her. So I gave her passing two or three days for the dust to settle and then one evening I just got quiet, tuned in, and visualized her. I was startled at how fast I found her. As long as I have my mental faculties, I won't forget the encounter.

With all the vibrant energy I had known her to have, she recognized me instantly. She was beaming and she looked like the

Lydia I remembered. I recall the sensation of there being a lot of others around her as well, while we were connecting. Sort of like a high-school reunion. The first thing she said to me was, "Are you here, too?" She was, of course, asking if I had transitioned also. Obviously I told her that no, I was still in the physical but had learned to bounce back and forth. Lydia relayed to me that she was excited to be where she was. She had been so confused for so many years and hadn't enjoyed the condition. She had no regrets and she wasn't looking back. She had been very devout while physical and I think she felt this was the reward for the fruit of her labors.

I went out of my way to thank her for contacting me after my divorce and tried to convey how much it had meant to me at the time. Then I asked her how she was seeing me. I had been curious when we project to the other side, how we're perceived. What do we look like to those already over there? Are we dust, or vapor, or what?

She was surprised at my question and said emphatically, "Why, you're standing right in front of me!" Once again, Lydia had saved me, in a sense. I had asked the question of the universe many times about the process as we teleport and Lydia helped me get the answer.

So my truth at this point is we mentally send ourselves across the fence by visualizing. Even if we just make up the appearance of a desired person or entity energetically, we can get ourselves to the right mail box.

And it appears that in our mental projection, we arrive and are perceived as 3D to whomever or whatever is on the other side. That's an amazing process.

Everything is energetic and a simple projected thought to the non-physical creates form. Of course! It's so simple. I had heard the theory before, but the encounter with Lydia was a huge conformation to me. Thanks again, Lydia.

DIVINE INTERVENTION

Gabe, did you want to enter here?

It would be good for you to share another few of your experiences. Others will be able to relate. We will stand in the background and watch over your shoulder.

Okay, Gabe, I'll take it away. Don't go too far, though.

The following stories are a result of my tendency to be over-confident at times and generally in a hurry to get things done. Thankfully through all my speedy ways, something has had my back. Over the years it took several experiences to start to see the pattern. Look what I'd have missed out on if I hadn't been so impetuous.

Before I got into the plumbing world, I did a lot of handy man work which later led to the plumbing. On this occasion a customer needed some new wiring replaced in an air conditioner mounted on a roof. The job wasn't something I normally got into, but it was straight forward and I knew I could do it.

Air conditioners draw a lot of electrical current. And they have big switches in place so they can be de-energized for repairs. They also have what is called a disconnect box right at the base of the unit. It's there so that if the AC has to be serviced, it can be conveniently disabled right then and there. It saves a trip back down to the main electric panel.

To start this wiring project, I needed to turn off the circuit breakers that fed the disconnect box. These breakers are the on-off switches that are located in the electric panel essentially for the whole house. I made sure the right circuit breakers were off to the AC unit on the roof and went back up and pulled the disconnect switch. There. Now the unit was out of service. I could begin the rewiring related to the disconnect. Next all I had to do was to take a screwdriver and detach the old wiring in the disconnect box so I could remove and replace it. I confidently selected the appropriate screwdriver and located the first of the necessary screws.

Just as the tip of my screwdriver started to contact the screw, there was a mental twist in my brain. It was like my head had been squeezed. I didn't know what caused it, but I realized it was happening and my arm connected to the hand with the screwdriver jerked in such a way that the tip of the screwdriver missed the intended screw. The screwdriver basically over shot the entire connection I had aimed at. It was as if I had an ice cream cone in my hand and as I went to bring it up to my mouth and missed and hit the center of my forehead. It was that much of a reaction.

Well that little event got my attention. I was dumbfounded and started to ponder what had just taken place, and for some reason I just knew that the screw I was headed for was still connected to a very electrified wire. I got some other tools out that could verify my thinking and sure enough, the wire I had started to disconnect was highly charged with electrical current. I did figure out what the malfunction was and remedied the situation.

The point here is that the squeezed mental sensation had never happened to me before or since in that way. All I can surmise is that there was energy around me that knowingly intervened. I don't know how it did, what it did, or how it knew to do what it did. I've never had any etheric confirmation about the event. At this point, it's all my own conjecture. The only downside of the situation was I missed out on being able to glow in the dark.

I am finding your tale amusing, Scott. For there is a casual tone about your story that is complacent, in a sense.

You did not accurately convey your astonishment at the fact that you had come so close to an out-of-body experience. Possibly one on a permanent basis. It was rather, shall we say, earth-shattering for you. You have not felt that engaged about being on the edge since then. We applaud your steadfast ability to downplay your adventures. Continue on.

Scott, may we suggest that you realize the importance of what you have just discussed.

In what way, Gabe?

Scott, the value in this story is to understand to what extent you were being watched over and cared for. There is no need to dissect the process, just know that it is there watching over you every moment. There is vigilance in place that is always alert to help keep you out of harm's way. In this story, you did not see the help coming, but it was there nonetheless. Your next story illustrates your awareness of the alert that came your way and you took advantage of the call.

This next story gives new meaning to the term, 'Bumper to Bumper.' I had arrived at a job one day and there were other tradesmen working on the house when I pulled up. For some reason I was standing in the street between the bumpers of two parked cars to get a perspective I needed on the house and what I was there to do. As I was processing my situation and standing between these two cars, a young woman came out of the house. She was walking with intent and from the way she was dressed, I assumed she was headed to work. I went on scanning the house and conversing with my customer a short distance away. Meanwhile this young lady got in the car to my right.

So there I was in the front of the car she got into and at the rear of the car to my left. There was just enough room for me to stand comfortably between the bumpers of these two cars. As the door closed on the car to my right, I had the thought, "What if she starts the car and it lurches forward? It could happen, but what are the odds?" Next I had the thought, "What the heck, I'll just play it safe." So I took two steps backward into the center of the street to move out from between the bumpers and went on with my scanning. Just as I did that, the lady in her car to my right put her key in the ignition and started the engine. As the engine came to life, guess what, the car lurched forward! Had I remained where I was standing, I'd have had my legs rearranged at bumper level.

She managed to stop the lurching of her car just before it hit the car in front of her that had been on my left. However, she had a look on her face that conveyed terror over what could have happened to me had I decided to stay put. She was clearly aware of where I was standing and she registered my backward movement. It was one of those close calls, as they say.

What was strange to me at the time, because I remember seeing how scared she was after the fact, was how totally unaffected I was. Actually, I even remember sort of smirking and laughing to myself. I wasn't startled or angry. I was at peace because I had seen it coming.

For some reason, in that encounter I was warned and I responded. I have to wonder just how many warnings I hear, as opposed to how many I ignore. If I look back on my life, I'd say the number of warnings I have waved off far outnumber the ones I've heard and complied with.

So Gabe, I'm wondering in the case of the bumpers, was that just life experience on my part having lived X numbers of years or was I being warned?

It was a little of both. We would call it an easy save. It was easy for the universe to essentially warn you because there was life experience on your part to work with. The universe stimulated recall in you that made you aware of possibilities. In this case, you caught the signal the universe was sending. This time you listened and were proactive, as opposed to being complacent and thinking, "Oh that will not happen." This time you had the sense to consider the possibilities.

In the event with the air conditioner, you had no real warning to tap into because you were focused on the task at hand and were blocking transmissions. The guardian energy around you had to step up its game and got involved on another level to disrupt the possibilities. You could have chosen to attempt to loosen the screw again and just waved off the jerk of your arm to an, "Oops." But your awareness channel kicked in and you took a second look at the situation. Do you see? The universal energy has a lot of options to deal with. Fortunately for you, most of the time you pay attention to your tuner.

There was true interaction at the universal level for you in both of those situations. There is a third experience you should relate. It is pertinent here as well. That would be the story of the airplane trip from Colorado.

We have the feeling that the next story would best illustrate the universe in action. In that situation, you ignored the signals and the universe responded and helped you, anyway.

Gabe, is the story you're speaking of about Danny's plane?

Yes.

The experience Gabe speaks of had its beginning during my first years as an airline flight attendant. While I was doing that, I developed a strong interest in learning to fly airplanes myself. I realized that airline pilots at the time made a lot more money than flight attendants. The airline I was working for was facing a turnover situation with a lot of retiring pilots in the upcoming years. So I thought that since I already worked for the airline, if I could get the training to fly, then I might be in the right place at the right time. With the goal of a higher income in mind and the seeming adventure of flying for a living, I jumped head first into taking flight training and doing anything I could think of to get in an airplane and accumulate flight hours and experience.

About the middle of the six years I spent chasing airplanes, I had an in-law who had bought what could have been considered an antique plane. It wasn't a relic exactly, but it was about 35 years old when Danny bought it. He was dabbling in flying small planes but was not on the mission I was.

When Danny bought the plane I'm speaking of, it was in Colorado and Danny needed it flown to Southern California. I offered to go get the plane and bring it to him. I could go to Colorado and fly it to Phoenix, where I lived, and then take it to San Diego after that. It was a great opportunity for some free flying and it would be a new place to go see and explore.

I arranged travel and got myself to Colorado and found the little airport where the plane was located.

I was young and invincible. Considering all the factors, regarding the age and unknown mechanical condition of the plane, I shouldn't have put my body in that airplane and taken off. I had no history with that craft. It had been sitting for some time and I didn't know what worked on the plane and what didn't. I didn't know when it had last been mechanically inspected and I didn't know if its paperwork was in order that made it legal to fly. I didn't care. I just wanted to fly.

I blindly justified my intent to do this flight and started my preflight check. I did all the normal looking that one is taught to do before getting in any plane prior to flight. I made sure all the exterior nuts and bolts were in the right place and that the wheels were attached. I checked the fuel and oil along with the condition of the wooden propeller. Feeling satisfied with the exterior of the plane, I climbed in and got settled and started the engine to see what would happen next.

It fired up! That was another very cool thing to me. I let the engine warm up and just started making myself familiar with what few instruments there were in the plane. The vintage age of the plane was awesome to me. It was like going back in time some 35 years.

Okay, the plane looked good. Check. The plane started. Check. The fuel gauges read full. Check. I visually inspected the fuel tanks. Check. The oil pressure gauge was indicating normal. Check. Amp meter gauge showed the plane was producing electric power. Check. The flight controls were all free and work correctly. What more could I ask for?

What I should have asked for was what the weather conditions in the Phoenix area were going to be around the time I was planning on reaching that part of the trip.

To further qualify my intent to make this flight, I pushed in the throttle enough to make this classic craft start to move and I pulled away from the parking area. I was having a blast. I just taxied around the airport going up and down the rows of parked planes and around the hangars, getting a feel for the plane and seeing if it would keep running. I did that until I felt the need to get going.

The next thing one does before takeoff is to go to the end of the runway and hold the brakes. Those worked. Check. After you have the brakes set, you accelerate the engine to a specified speed, shown by the tachometer. You then proceed to inspect some other components of the engine by flipping some switches off and on to see how the engine reacts. There are some things the engine is supposed to do and some things the engine is not supposed to do when completing this last engine check. In this case, the engine did what it was supposed to do. Check. Nothing left now but call the tower and tell them I was ready to go. I said, "I'm ready;" the tower said, "Go," and I did. I pushed in the throttle to its full position and thought about Charles Lindbergh as I heard the engine rev up. The plane began to roll and gain speed as I started my historic flight from a little airport in Colorado to a big airport in San Diego. "Ah, here I am back in time, flying a plane with a wooden propeller, winging my way through the countryside. It doesn't get any better than this, unless you have working navigation equipment."

I turned to the southwest with my flight map open and on my lap for this leg of the trip. I was planning to get to Phoenix around eight o'clock the first night.

This trip was being made way before there was GPS so flight training involved in learning to use aerial maps. Okay, I knew how to do that. And I had a VOR to back me up. That's a flight direction system that utilizes aviation transmitters on the ground. You tune into the stations and the instrument in the plane tells you which way to go to get to that particular station. On the flight map, the stations are listed and plotted so you know where you are in reference to them, along with the map in your lap. That is, if your VOR is working.

I couldn't check this VOR on the ground before I left. I had to be up in the air where the VOR could receive signals. This unit in Danny's plane turned on so I could set the frequency, but the needle wouldn't lock on to the station I tuned to; it just lazily swung back and forth. No big deal; the sky was clear. I had my map and knew how to use it. The flight would continue.

I followed railroads and highways until I got lost and had no idea where I was. I wondered if this happened to Mr. Lindbergh. I had a compass in the plane and just continued southwest, figuring I'd have to run into a city of some kind somewhere. I still kept trying to orient my map to the ground and terrain, and eventually found out where I was.

Not being familiar with this plane, I didn't know how fast it would go and I didn't know how much gas it burned in a given amount of time. Typically, this is need-to-know information that's important so you can plan to not run out of gas. You can't just pull over and fill up in the sky. I don't remember what I did, in planning for fuel stops. I was just going to land when I saw the fuel gauges looking low and fuel up. Once fueled, I could measure the gallons used against the hours flown and then I'd have a better idea of how long I could safely let the plane stay in the air.

As I had roughly calculated, I got into northern Arizona around dark. I really enjoy flying at night. The lights in the cities below are mesmerizing. You can see the cars on the highways. And then there are all the stars. It's also easier to see other aircraft and the birds are all asleep. Flying at night has its drawbacks, however, and that's if you have to make an emergency landing, you aren't able to pick out landing spots easily, if at all.

As night fell on this first day of the flight, I came into northern Arizona and I could see the rotating airport beacon of an airport known as St. Johns. There's a VOR transmitter located at this airport that I could have taken advantage of if the VOR receiver in the plane had been working correctly.

This part of Arizona is at a higher elevation of the state where it's forested and not heavily populated. I had landed at this airport before for fuel so I was familiar with it and its proximity to Phoenix and home. In a flying sense, I didn't have much farther to go to get to Phoenix. In a way the rest of the trip was all downhill from St. Johns to home for the night. The wooded and mountainous terrain would be falling as I got closer to the Phoenix valley.

Excellent! I was on the short end of the trip. I had two fuel tanks that read to be each half full. I didn't have far to go and there was enough gas to get home. The engine hadn't missed a beat and I was on a mental high flying at night. Ahhhmazing. The only thing that could improve my situation was to experience a moonlit flight on top of a solid cloud layer completely devoid of any land marks for reference. And there it was!

Feeling that I didn't need gas, I over flew St. Johns and headed for Phoenix. As I pushed on I could sometimes see the beacon at St. Johns airport out the rear of the plane. Now that I think about it, I don't know why I felt the need to look out the back of the plane. It seemed like I wasn't pulling away from St. Johns as fast as I should have been. In other words, the over-flown airport wasn't disappearing in the rearview mirror.

As I got closer to the Phoenix area, I started to experience this amazing picture in front of me of a perfectly flat calm layer of clouds that was definitely below me. The moon was big and round and ahead of me to the west. The moonlight was lighting up the cloud layer below and, because of the angle of the moon, light shadows were created in the texture of the clouds. I was thinking it was pretty and scary at the same time, but what the heck.

As I mentioned, I hadn't checked on weather conditions in the Phoenix area. I wasn't concerned because I had just been there the same morning. So somehow, some way, since I'd left Phoenix this huge low-level cloud layer moved in and completely covered the place.

"Okay, now I need a plan. This plane isn't equipped to fly through clouds. Okay, no big deal; I'll just push on and find a hole in the cloud layer and pop through. Okay, that's the plan." The problem with this plan was I knew I was over high country with a lot of trees, but I didn't know if the clouds were ABOVE the trees or IN the trees. You don't want to just pop through clouds into one of those tall pines. That can be very unforgiving.

As I was continuing with my recently-hatched plan, I could see two glowing areas in the clouds ahead of me. There was one straight ahead and one off to the left, at about 12 o'clock and 10 o'clock. They were like big flashlights shining through a white blanket from underneath. Of course the illuminated areas in the clouds were from the cities below. The good news was cities and civilizations were ahead. The bad news was I didn't know which cities they were.

I figured the lights straight ahead were Phoenix and the lights on the left were Tucson to the south of Phoenix. Even if I was right about the cities and their locations, I still couldn't get down through the clouds. And now my fuel gauges weren't showing two times half full. They were showing two times empty and St. Johns was too far away to try to go back. Holy you-know-what! How did I get myself into this?

I was starting to sweat. I panicked and futurized a vision of what Danny's plane would look like in a tree – not even my plane and I had destroyed it. "Okay. I have to shake that picture." My heart rate was definitely elevated. Back to mind. Scanning and scanning. "I need a new plan. Check fuel gauges again. They're still looking empty. Okay, save gas. Pull back the power and fly as slowly as possible. That will let me think. Try the VOR again, just maybe. Tune in Phoenix frequencies from the map. Damn. The needle is just swinging. No lock." Back to mental scanning and scanning. "Okay, no choices; try arrival frequencies. Maybe they can find me on radar and direct me."

I put out a call on the radio with the aircraft call sign. Then I heard, "Aircraft calling Williams towers (Williams Air Force base), go ahead." I responded, "Williams, this is aircraft so-and-so. I'm in need of direction to nearest airport. My location is between St. Johns and Phoenix." Williams returned, "Aircraft so-and-so squawk (a term for a numeric code that's given by the tower for me to enter into a radio on the plane that puts out a signal that radar can better see)." Shoot, the transponder wouldn't turn on. So I replied to Williams as if I had complied just to make it all look good.

The tower I was in communication with was basically telling me that they couldn't find me. Just as they were in the middle of trying to help, me I looked over to my left and saw the only hole in the clouds below that existed that night. I wanted to say it was the size of a dinner plate. It was probably bigger than that, but it was the only hole in the clouds that I had seen. I was initially in disbelief. Through the hole, I could see blue taxiway lights at the edge of a runway.

"SERIOUSLY? THIS IS INSANE! What are the odds that I'm out of gas on top of clouds that I don't dare descend through because of terrain and trees below, and I find the one hole in the clouds that reveals an airport below it?" I processed this all in a nanosecond, realizing it meant I was definitely not over trees, but a real airport. "If I just put the plane in a slow circular spiral and do it right this instant so I don't stray from this point, I should be able to circle though the cloud layer and break out on top of that airport." I didn't have any other choice so I did just that.

Over the radio I told the tower I was talking to that I had some runway lights in sight and was going to land and then I focused on the plane. I started a gentle spiral to the left and the windshield went blank as I went through the clouds. Without any visual orientation, I just held the gentle bank and what only took 30 seconds seemed like 30 minutes. My slight spiral brought me out of the cloud layer and, make no mistake, there it was in all its radiant glory – a fully lit taxiway right next to a runway. Hallelujah! The cloud layer was now above me and I could see the ground below; in fact it was high enough over the airport to give me plenty of maneuvering room. Without delay, I oriented the plane, got aligned with the runway, and landed with the engine still running.

OMG! What were the chances of all of that happening? It was surreal. There was no one to high-five with and there were no cheering crowds lined up on the ramp. There was just me and my space ship. That was it. Not that I would have planned it but wow, what a rush that was. I'm still dazed and amazed to think about it.

I regrouped and found out where I was – Globe, Arizona. It's a small historic town related to the copper mines of the area. The road from Phoenix to St. Johns goes right by this little airport. I found a pay phone and called the after-hour number for the fuel truck to come out and gas me up. Then I called my wife and told her where I was and that she could pick me up at the airport near our home in an hour. With a sigh of relief and full tanks again, I took off from Globe and stayed under the cloud layer as I made a beeline for the airport near my house. My wife was there to pick me up and all was well. At that point, I could let go of the image of Danny's plane in a tree.

Just to fill in the aftermath of this flight the next day, I found out that as I left St. Johns and headed to Phoenix, I had unknowingly flown into 50-mph winds. Head wind to a plane is a little like a boat trying to move forward in the water while dragging an anchor. If you're in a plane that says you're going 100 mph in the air, and you're flying into a 50-mph head wind, you're actually only going to be going 50 mph over the ground. That's why when I was leaving St. Johns, it seemed like it was taking a long time to actually get down the road. I was flying full speed ahead and really getting nowhere fast, burning up my fuel.

Okay, Gabe, I was practically reliving that experience as I was writing about it. Is this the story you had in mind for me to tell about?

Yes, Scott, it was exactly the story we wanted you to share. It is pertinent to how the universe protects those who are tuned in, versus those who are not. In your case your channel was not as open to receiving as it usually is. Reception was overridden by your exuberance for engaging in the flying adventure. It is very typical of humans to disregard connection in light of wants and achievements of immediate gratification.

Your focus on your adventure was not a bad thing; it just would have been less tumultuous for you had you knowingly tuned in and LISTENED TO WHAT WAS BEING SENT. You, like a very young child, put all your focus on the desire of the moment. That can be dangerous if you do not hear the warning shots. You managed to learn many valuable lessons on this trip. It was not a wasted event in your life.

Before you ask the question, we know your next thought. You are wondering what really saved you from harm on that night. You want to think that something outside of you came to your rescue. You feel that the odds of the outcome turning out the way it did were simply impossible. It does not seem right to you that you were saved by simple, dumb luck. It makes more sense to you that something outside of you

211

and larger and more powerful was responsible for seeing you to safety.

Yes, Gabe, my dreamy fantasy side would love to have that be what happened. That possibility is something that I've always hoped was true and wanted to be true, but the concept has not been categorically proven to me. I always have my doubts. I don't count on it being the case. I'd like to think that some guiding hand gently pushed the plane over to and on top of the little airstrip below and then parted the clouds for me to see my way to a safe landing. I'm just not settled thinking it simply worked out. There were too many things that had to come together. Then on the other hand, it seems absurd to think that little ol' me had the power and did save myself. It's endearing to maybe think there were angels under each wing pushing me to safety when I didn't have a clue where I was.

As I was noting empty fuel tanks, I certainly wasn't aware of communicating with anything other than my own fears in the moment. I felt very alone in the minutes before landing. It's funny; as glad as I was to be safe on the ground, at the same time I was in disbelief that things had turned out so well for me.

Some thinking that I've had over the years about this flying experience is that, "Okay, I was lucky enough to make it out of that mess." But that doesn't explain the many stories about those that don't make it out of such a self-inflicted situation as I got myself into. I wonder why I made it and they didn't. Why does one man not make it back from the battlefield and another comes back unscathed? I'm looking to see if there's a process in place that I can learn to use or tap into that I can count on 100% of the time. I always want to be the guy walking back from the battlefield unscathed. It just doesn't make sense to me, if there's a caring energy that surrounds us all, why some are chosen to come back and others don't make it. There has to be something that I don't understand.

It does make sense on a universal level, Scott. That is what you must understand. There is, as you say, a bigger picture. The picture is so big that you would not understand it even if we laid out the process for you. You, even with your inquisitive side, cannot fathom the dynamic energies that are intertwining even as we speak.

There are reference points that may help you that can be explained, but we could never paint the entire picture for you to see. That is something that you just have to know is there. It would not serve you to try to understand the entirety of universal operation, when all you really need to understand is that, generally speaking, there is energy around you that looks out for you.

In anticipation of your next question, even this energy cannot save you if you ignore the warnings and get yourself too deep in a situation where there is no way out. It is like rock climbing. Sometimes you can climb into a crevice where you have not planned your exit and you find that you cannot get yourself back out. Does that make sense?

Scott, having said that to you, what saved you was YOU! Your experience and your curiosity for life gave you knowledge to draw upon. The universe had a library to tap into and guide you by calling up those moments from the past that you could recall and utilize. You drew in energy that helped you keep calm and rational. Had you gone into stark raving panic mode, the outcome might have been different.

You were staggered at the coincidence of being on top of an airport when you needed one. Were the chances astronomical? Yes, they certainly were. In that situation your energy guidance system was tuned to the maximum signal strength. Your focus sent an S.O.S. message loud and clear, and the universe responded. Had you cowered and withdrawn into fear, your signal strength would not have generated the attention of the energy that responded. If you want to call what came to your rescue as angelic or divine, so be it. The troops to the rescue all come from the same source.

You are the driver of the bus! Get that concept down. It is important to know that you and all other humans are sitting behind the wheel of your life. Some are more suited to driving than others and that is okay. At some point, those in the back seat will want to move to the front. We applaud those who want to stomp on the gas pedal and we applaud those who want to just hang on for the ride. It is perfectly okay which energy you choose. Just understand that the one with the steering wheel in their hands has more options at their immediate disposal.

Those riding along behind the driver are more likely to stumble and have trouble getting up when the occasion arises. That is all right, as well.

Remember the seat you are in was chosen by you. You can drive or you can sit and ride. It is that simple.

Gabe, in looking at my escape from possible misfortune as you suggest, to accept that I saved myself sort of takes all the fun out of it. It's much more interesting to think that something outside of me was caring for me and was there to perform the rescue.

For certain, Scott it is much more comforting to think there is someone else that will clean up the dishes after the meal. But for the most part, it is the person eating off the plate who is responsible for cleaning it and putting it away.

Another view you might consider is if you do not want that responsibility, you do not even need the plate. You can eat with your hands. Even less responsible would be thinking someone else should put the food in your mouth and chew it for you. That way you do not need to even wash your hands.

Humanity is reaching a point in its evolution where there is chronic expectation that someone else should drive the bus and take them exactly where they want to go. It does not work like that. Life in the physical is not always easy. But you chose it. Sorry. You can delude yourself for as long as you wish. No rush. You have eternity to figure it out. Be as deluded as you wish for as long as you wish. That is okay.

In a sense, Gabe, I don't enjoy what you're telling me. It throws me out of alignment on the belief structure I've created to this point to justify my existence. I know that generally one doesn't want their beliefs shaken up because it creates discomfort. People don't want to be uncomfortable and tend to cling to what they know.

Yes, we would agree with you, but understand that discomfort can be a valuable tool. It makes you look in other directions while you are trying to regain being comfortable. While you are looking for the remedy to comfort you, inevitably you grow on some level. That is the tool of the universe. It is a tool we do not purposely use, but to those willing to explore the edge of what they know and believe, it becomes a common process. You have entered the discomfort zone many times. Sometimes willingly and sometimes you had no intention of having the encounter. The trick is that during those unintended encounters with discomfort, you take advantage of the moment. As has been said, do not let a good crisis go to waste.

I know I'll continue to process what you have just presented and work to find a new comfort zone, but what I really want you to give me is a rendition about all of this that could be presented to a child. What could I tell a child who is curious about what's going on in the universe? How could I explain to a child that he or she will have to count on saving himself from harm and keep his wits about himself?

Gabe, do you see what I mean? Someone is going to ask and I'd like to have a kind, loving answer and example to convey.

There is no kind, loving, simple answer we can give you except to say that the universe is dripping with energetic options that can be at one's finger tips in an instant. You can use whatever label you want to in describing this energy. You can call this energy a thing or see it as a translucent light. You could even see it as a red dragon named Leroy. There are many cultures and many beliefs in place where you live. It does not matter what culture is in focus or what term people in that culture use for deities and belief structures.

All cultures and beliefs are accessing the same energetic energy. That is what is important to know. As for what you could say to a child, simply tell them they are responsible for their own life and plant the seed early. That is the most honest thing you can say. Let them know that you are always there to support them and assistance is available in many forms. They need to know, however, that ultimately they decide their own solutions. Let your children know that all they have to do in any situation is to simply get quiet, ask, and listen to the knowing that is inside.

The essence of what you want to convey is that there is helping, caring energy all around them that will help guide them for their highest good. Then while they grow, they will learn to take responsibility for their own actions. Children will do more with that teaching than you might think. It is not in anyone's best interest to teach them that there is an energy that will save them from self-inflicted consequences.

Think of a dam that is holding back enough water to create a lake. Let us say the dam is a situation in your life that you unsuspectingly become interested in or aware of. As you approach the dam, you note a leak in the structure. Think of the leak as a call to become aware of what you have going on around you. You can note the leak and take action to repair it before it gets worse, or you can distract yourself, ignore the signals, and wait for someone else to deal with the leak. If the leak is ignored, eventually the crack will get worse and the dam could break and the lake will drain. If you act and take action early, then you might be able to still plug the hole with the help of the universe. However, if you wait too long, the leak might become too large to fix. When you wait too long to ask for help, the problem becomes too serious for even the universe to help. The universe can be called in at any time. But at some point, if the signs have been ignored too long, the universe cannot bring enough remedy to the matter soon enough. Does that make sense?

For example, a woman looking in the mirror one day notices an abnormality in her breast. At first she does not believe what she is seeing. "This cannot be," might be her thought. She has just noted the crack in her dam. Now she can ignore what she is seeing and mentally delude herself with thoughts like, "Oh, it is nothing. It will go away." Or she can be proactive then and there, and commit to investigating further and having this abnormality checked out.

Some days later this woman is at the grocery store doing necessary shopping. She is pushing her cart through the store and happens to hear two women conversing about breast cancer. She notes the conversation but says to herself, "That will not happen to me," and continues shopping.

Some time passes and the condition has escalated. (The crack in her dam is allowing more water to flow out). She is out in her car and notices an advertisement for a breast cancer walk near her home. This makes her think of her own breast issue and she thinks to herself, "Oh maybe I should have it looked at," but languishes further and does not make the call. Ultimately her condition is so obvious that her husband takes note. Being mindful and concerned, he insists that she get to a doctor as soon as possible.

By the time all this has occurred, her condition has worsened to the point that it is now necessary for her to endure extreme measures to try to correct her issue. Treatment commences but in the end it was too late. The break in the dam had been ignored too long and it ultimately burst.

There was the morning she first noted the problem in the mirror. Then there was the day she overheard the conversation at the grocery store. Finally she saw the advertisement for the cancer walk. These were all calls from the universe to guide her for her best good. Had she taken heed of the warnings, her dam might not have burst. The universe was trying to get her attention and guide her. Ultimately, though, the action that needed to be taken was her responsibility.

Scott, this would be the most kind and gentle way of conveying to another how the universe works.

Gabe, this story sounds a lot like what a friend of mine went through some years ago. Her name was Deb.

We thought you might note the similarity.

This story about, let us say Deb, can be compared to your flying experience. You had doubt when you looked back and noted the over-flown airport was not disappearing behind you. (You noted a crack in your dam). That was a warning. You flew on, anyway. You became uncomfortable when you unexpectedly encountered never-ending cloud cover that you were not prepared to deal with. (That was the dam cracking further). This discomfort was a warning. You flew on, anyway.

You could say the third call was the hole in the clouds, when you allowed yourself to be rescued. After tapping on your shoulder two other times God/the universe came to protect you on the third round, before the dam burst. Do you see?

Yes, I do. Your story is very clear to understand and I get it. And I thank you. I tend to be obsessed by wondering about things like who showed up and what the process that took place in the rescue was. I have a little bit of engineer mentality in me. In a way I'm still the little boy who wants to catch Santa in the act.

We heartfully understand and we can see the hurt your inner child continues to react to. Just know the process is energetic and that you command it. It is like turning on a light switch. You just turn it on when you need it.

You know that if you flip a light switch, the light goes on or off. You do not stop to think about the wire in the wall or the power plant that is generating the electricity. When you move the switch, you are not concerned with the tradesman that originally installed the switch in the wall. You have just come to know that the switch will turn the light on or off.

For the sake of reinforcement, suppose on a given night you are walking down a dark hall and several times you bump into a wall or door.

Consider those bumps as shots over the bow. The bumps become warnings that you should turn on the light. If you do not find the switch, you might fall down a stairwell as a result. And that would be okay. You would learn something from the experience. Or after the first bump, you could reach for the switch. It is your choice.

Gabe, it's hard to know when to reach for the switch. You tend to think that the first bump is nothing but an 'oops.' You don't realize that you're being warned. Then you get another bump and you're focused on a task and say, "What the heck." So you push on your way, still not thinking you're being warned. You say to yourself, "I'm having a crazy day," and keep going. So I'm saying that I know I've missed warning shots before, not on purpose but just because I was engaged with life and not connecting the dots. So I guess what I'm wondering about is how does one categorically know when to be aware they're being warned?

Scott, it is a task at hand for the individual to learn the signs, develop a focus, and pay attention.

There is a bit of a conspiracy going on here. Life teaches you to become aware, whether you are conscious or not. Life does not give up on you. It keeps sending the warnings one after another, much like an automatic baseball pitching machine. And if you keep missing the signals, life just keeps sending them your way regardless. Eventually you do learn to see the pattern.

Do not confuse life warnings with life-learning situations. There is a difference. Sometimes they come singularly and sometimes they come in the same package.

One way or another, the contents of the package will cause you to maneuver differently. You learn to do things another way.

Learning to eat spaghetti is an example of learning to maneuver differently. The first time you were presented with the opportunity to eat this food, you probably used your hands and got most of it on your face and chair tray and the floor. As you got older and were given more chances to savor the dish, you got better at finding ways to get it to its intended journey's end. And you eventually evolved to where you were unceremoniously able to eat the pasta noodles without getting sauce all over everything.

Now as for warnings, those usually will come from within. It is the little voice inside that is saying, "This is not a good idea." Or the feeling that something is wrong or at least not right. You might get the jitters about something or a nagging thought that you should check on a situation or verify a planned result. Then it is the conscious decision to take action that needs to come into play next.

Alerts about considering taking action or choosing another way of being come in many forms. It does not even have to be in a physical event. Cautions can come in the form of an internal feeling or a mindful knowing or words from someone near you. The trick is to perceive through whatever source is your strong side and stay awake and aware.

When you are using a map looking for your destination, you are focused on the task of reaching your end point. You are looking for land marks or signs that correlate with the map. You are in the moment of knowing where you are and where you want to be. You are conscious of barriers that may require you to make another turn that you were not expecting. That kind of focus is what you want to develop and be empowered with. The past does not matter; it is over. What is coming is not of concern because it will not matter until you get there. Where you are right now is your focus point. Maintain your focus on where you are putting each foot print. That way you can avoid rough terrain on the first encounter.

So Gabe, you're saying learning to eat spaghetti is more of a practice at learning to get better at something. A warning is more like the feeling I had in Danny's plane when I realized the airport behind me was not fading in the distance like I thought it should.

Yes, in that case the feeling you had was a call to arms, in a sense. It was your inner knowing or universe hot-line at work. There was a wrinkle in the energy field trying to alert you to a possible malfunction. And in the aftermath that experience was profound enough that it also served as a learning situation as well. Having that event under your belt to draw on made you a safer pilot on future flights.

You got a two-for-one on that deal. You were the lucky one!

Section VI

God has entrusted me with myself.

Epictetus

JESUS PICKED UP THE TAB

This section was the last that I received. I got some of it at the very end of the last day of the writing seminar and then more over the next few days after I arrived home. I relay the following with some hesitation only because I don't see myself as a Bible thumper and I don't agree with the hell-fire and damnation processes. I don't view myself as a chosen one or a sentinel from God to carry the message of righteousness. That's just not my gig.

I feel better now that I have qualified my position and I can go on. One afternoon, as I was doing some tweaking on this book, whatever the energy is that's working with me said I'd have a visitor in my dreams with a message that the world could bear to hear.

Now I know what Ebenezer Scrooge felt like with all the ghosts showing up for him. I didn't disregard the message. I just put it off to the side in my head and thought, "Okay, that would be nice. Yeah, all right," and went back to what I was doing.

So on the following Friday night, two days after receiving my prophesy, I got home late from work. The family was on a brief trip to California and I had the house to myself.

I did the brush-my-teeth thing, turned out the light, got in bed, and landed my head on the pillow. I lay there, aware of being totally alone in the house. I didn't have to worry about anyone but me. I was enjoying how really quiet it was. Peace was surrounding me and then guess what, Jesus showed up.

This was not the first time it had happened to me. There've been other occasions in other places. Several times as a kid, I had these J encounters. Also, on occasion I've had the experience in Sedona. Maybe there's something in the water up there.

I was not startled at the arrival, just sort of surprised, and the connection was clear. I certainly wasn't expecting that level of the hierarchy to drop in.

Just to share, I have an ongoing game I play with Jesus. On many occasions I've sent out the invitation to have lunch with him. The lack of response would leave me feeling invalidated, like when you give your phone number to the opposite sex and say, "Call me," and they don't. Like the persistent suitor, though, I just kept sending the invite anyway. I think it would be amazing to sit down with the guy and just get his take on things, rather than what we've been told by prior generations.

As I became aware of the energy touching in, I had the thought, "Shoot, this couldn't be the lunch date; it's too late in the day."

Once I keyed in to his arrival, the vision started. When I first got into bed, I was on my right side. I was asked to turn onto my back, so I did. This tends to give me a better sense of the vision. As I turned over I climbed through the veil, as it were, and put myself in front of Jesus. He proceeded to kneel down and wash my feet like we hear about in the biblical tales. It was interesting. But I found myself feeling a little embarrassed, even in this vision. Still, I told myself to just register the experience and see what happened. It was only a vision, right?

Basically what transpired was that he had a message to give me to put out here. Oh, great, now I have to tell the world's religions that they have it all wrong. I can't see any barriers to deal with there.

I got quiet and heard Jesus start to connect.

Scott, you and I have connected more than once, as you recall. You can remember as a child, the encounter when I came to you after your mother had tried to explain what God was like. You stood still while I shared with you that you were part of me and that I would be with you.

Scott, you are a bright soul. I would never let you down. I am Jesus. I have always admired your willingness to participate in life. You continue to show up at all the events, even when you are uncomfortable. And you continue to work on your beingness and question your place in the universe. You continually update who you are and that is to your benefit. You were secure in your deviation from the norm in your thinking process. You continued to explore and you always desired to get to the source of any teachings. And you became comfortable asking to be allowed to perceive the highest connection. You felt no need to shrink in the corner, as it were, in the presence of spiritual greats.

You have been seen and noticed. I am here to applaud you in your tenacity of spirit-bound connection.

Thank you, Sir. I'm always humbled when I encounter your energy. Thank you for dropping by. I apologize in advance for sharing what just went through my mind. It's late and you have shown up to talk. As you entered my energy, my mind went to what it would be like if you arrived at the set of a late-night talk show.

"Good evening, everyone. Welcome, ladies and gentleman. We have an interesting show for you tonight. We have a lot in store for you and we think you're going to really enjoy what we've planned. So sit back, relax, and enjoy the show."

"Our first guest is someone that you have all heard of and many of you have actually called out to him. He's touched hearts all over the world. Without further ado, ladies and gentleman, put your hands together for the one, the only, Jesus." (Then I wondered if there would be tumultuous applause or quiet hesitant response).

Good evening to you, sir. Thank you so much for being on my show. I know you are a busy guy. I'm sure the audience is all warmed up and anxious to hear what you have to say.

I enjoyed the way you presented me, Scott. I have never had an introduction like that before. I think I will have to have that used for me the next time I am playing at the Sistine Chapel. That kind of opening takes all the serious energy out of the presentation. I think that kind of introduction would help everyone relax a little and be more open to what I am trying to get across. You know what I mean? This experience is supposed to be carefree and it can be.

So Scott, now that you have introduced me, let us talk a little about you.

Me? Jesus, that surprises me. I wanted you on the show tonight to share. You have a lot of influence, you know. I thought the show tonight was going to be about you and your message.

I can see where you would think that. Everyone waits for me to start delivering. You, on the other hand, want to know what makes me tick. I find that refreshing.

You have to remember that being influential is not always a walk in the park. I do not really come across as entertaining. I can do a pretty good job of making people feel uncomfortable when I show up. When I walk into the room, the fun sort of stops and everyone gets real quiet. People see me and they stop what they are doing and just stand there and look. You are one of the few who actually come on over and want to connect.

There is some truth to the joke about, "Look busy, Jesus is coming." Everyone sees me walk in and they start to feel guilty and they go back to the food table and try to act like they do not know I am there.

You know how it goes. Usually everyone wants me to parade around and quietly bestow blessings on them.

Most think of me as being quiet and shy. You do not get anywhere in heaven by being quiet and shy. There is a lot of competition for attention. You have to get loud and boisterous to be heard. There is not any job for a quiet guy like my image might suggest.

Jesus, I can truly appreciate your situation. But you always show up, rain or shine. I want to thank you for your continuing support. "Ladies and gentleman, we'll be back after the break."

Jesus, I do have some questions I'd like to ask you as long as you're here. (Now I'm conscious of being back in my bed.)

Certainly, Scott. Continue.

Who or what is the energy that was working with me, if not you? I'm sort of confused why you came in at this point of the book, rather than the beginning of the process. I'm not complaining, just trying to connect the flow that I'm receiving from the non-physical.

You receive well and had I shown up other than as I did, you would not have received me in the same way. You needed to feel you were being accessed by some other energy than me, because your resistance was high at the beginning of this project. You needed to hammer out some thinking that you would not have been oriented to do had you known it was me.

Showing up as an intermediary was less intimidating to you. It softened the blow, as it were. If I had popped in and said, "This is the Jesus show," it would have created a different context for your work. You are curious, my friend.

So for now, understand that who I am is not to be confused with worship or adulation. I cannot truly serve you or anyone else if you do not have a desire to be helped out of your current thinking process. I am only part of a very big universe and I am actually an intermediary in yours and others' lives.

You and others with your thinking see me as a friend to be consulted and are comfortable to connect on a one-to-one experience. It is important for those who are not aware to know that they can connect as well on their own. There does not have to be a middleman or interpreter to reach me or any other part of the universe.

Connection with me can be very casual and personal or it can be very ceremonial. You create the setting; I just play the part you cast me with. I am the consummate actor, you know. I can play whatever part is necessary for me to get through to you. You write the play and I play the part that works for you. How is that for an upbeat current use of modern verbiage? You did not think I could be so cool.

Sir, I can accept your cool side. It doesn't intimidate me. But others of more traditional beliefs might find your being so cool a bit on the side of blasphemy. I guess it's all how one looks at things. I can go with the cool, casual thing with no problem and still hear you, and then I assume there are others who would expect to see you as formal and aloof. Possibly even shaming and angry. But I don't see you that way.

Your way of viewing me is your experience. Each pair of eyes will see me differently.

Sir, may I ask, are you the arrival I was told about a few days ago?

Yes, Scott, I am the visitor you were told about. Does that cause you to feel like a prophet?

I'm not sure, sir. This all seems so biblical. Is this how all the prophets of past got their messages? I hardly feel on a par with them. The only connection that I can see is with a prophet is the letter 'P.' P also stands for 'plumbing.' I was just expecting a casual drop-in advisor of sorts, not one of the big guys. So now I'm feeling a little like I have been pulled over in traffic by a policeman and wondering why. So, how are things with you?

Everything with me is heavenly, of course. I thought I would drop in and connect with you, Scott. I like the dramatic entrance. I wanted this to be more than one of our casual encounters. I wanted to engage with you more than I have in the past. I was pre-announced so you would not be so startled upon my arrival. I did not want to turn on the siren and lights and frighten you.

That was thoughtful of you, Sir. So what brings you to my humble little life?

Scott, I wanted to take advantage of the messenger side of your personality.

Okay, now I'm feeling really on guard. And how does my messenger side fit in here. Do I have to hand out flyers?

No, Scott. Handing out flyers is certainly an option but not needed. I want you to tell a story of sorts.

Sir, I could do that. Stories seem to be enjoyed by all. But I don't really think of myself as a storyteller. I'm about as average as a human can get, on a lot of levels. I do have my talents, but being the guy that speaks for the heavens hasn't been on my resume.

Sir, I'm seeing a potential problem here. I admit that I always have felt that the title of messenger would be a fit for me. But with you in the mix, I'm feeling a little insecure about the process. Who am I to stand up and proclaim that I, Scott, am receiving messages from such as you and everyone should listen to my words? I am a very small piece of the puzzle. I hold no huge title. Who the heck is going to listen to what I have to say?

That is just why I came to you. You can be very powerful as a small piece of the puzzle. I do not necessarily need the consummate celebrity to spread my word. The universe seeks out the common spirit who forges ahead and keeps trying to expand. The spirit of the well-intended does a much better job of putting their heart in the message than the self-proclaimed authority. You, I trust to tell what needs to be told on any occasion. You will not filter the words. If I come to you and others, each of you extends your influence in your own pocket of the world. Your pooled efforts will reach and help the combined many to expand. It is not one soul's mission to move humanity. Trust me, Scott, I would not advise trying that process. It does not have a lot of perks. Small efforts on the part of a lot of souls do more good on many levels with a lot less consternation.

Okay. I feel much better knowing that I don't have to lead a charge, as it were. I just don't know what message it is that I am to deliver. I have my thoughts about that. I'm drawn to relaying to others on a personal level what guidance I can receive for them.

I am, however, a little shaky thinking that I could be a spokesman for you, sir. I'm not a celebrity on any level and yet you say that I chose to be part of the process of delivering.

Scott, you were thinking that you wanted to show others how to expand and benefit as you have. That is your way. You have always been a way-shower of a kind.

Sir, I'm having one of my 'I wonder' thoughts forming here and I have to ask a question. Previously you said that I chose to participate in this message thing. How did all of this come about? Did I really chose or did you pick me specifically? Or did I answer an ad and say, "Sign me up?"

The reason I ask, Sir, is because there are hundreds of thousands times hundreds of thousands of bibles in the world that supposedly carry your messages. What could I possibly have to tell the world? Not to mention the equivalent books of other religions and the messages put forth in them. The magnitude of what you suggest is taking my breath away. If I'm over-thinking this, let me know.

I'm getting a picture of myself wearing a sandwich board walking up and down the highway saying, "Jesus lives." I've seen that done. I also saw all the cars keep on going past the devotee wearing the sign. That's not a pretty picture for me. I'm wondering if I really want all the phone calls and heckling that such an action could generate.

Scott, you do not have to be concerned with your safety. My message to you will draw no one who is not ready to hear it. There will always be those who will disparage you because of their own discomfort, relative to their current belief system. That is a given. I, on the other hand, will tenderly give you words to enlighten and inspire. That is all. It will be a very gentle process, for sure.

You will be comfortable with the message I will impart to you. The message will be yours and it will be for those who vibrationally align with you. Those that are not ready for it will get other messages until they can hear yours. Do not be confused about your connection with me. As you grow intuitively, you will understand that your journey has not been an accident. You chose it.

I can appreciate that philosophy, Sir. I'm still wrestling with the, 'I chose' thing. To hear you tell me that my journey has not been an accident, well, that sort of stops me in my tracks. I'm wondering what the heck I was thinking. I'm one little human on planet Earth. So I'm just one of eight billion who chose to talk to you and deliver your messages. How can that be?

Scott, it can be because you wanted the job. And remember this task of forwarding the message is not as daunting as you might think. You are one of millions who convey and reach those who are on your frequency. You are not alone. There are others just like you doing what you are doing. It is a combined effort. You will tell your story and mine with your talents, and others will do the same.

As for when you chose the task at hand, 'long ago' would be the simple answer. You are a career messenger, of sorts. Life after life, it has been your longing, and at times you spoke and you were punished for how you saw things. Other times you were embraced. Your cautious side is prevalent because in the past you became fearful to speak out due to repercussions. It is not unusual for one to hesitate to act when they are fearful of retribution. You have persisted and played it safe at times to survive. It is okay. The pendulum swings both ways. Now you can produce the message at hand and not be fearful of degradation. I am here at your side. Be my sound and know that I am the source. You can make me the fall guy. Truly. It will make things easier for you.

Sir, I'll see what I can do. So I have to ask, what does this message-giving look like? Also, is it time for me to ask, just what the message is that I need to hear and send out?

The message will be forthcoming. Let us first address another of your concerns.

Scott, I sense your hesitation for my selection of verbiage. You are thinking that I do not sound like a god.

My question to you, Scott, is, "What should a god sound like?" You accept my choice of words. However, you think others will not feel that my words are real if they do not have a particular vernacular. I will say this, that if I were to sound like a god, which I am not, with booming angry tones, some would hear the message but many more would turn away and depart. You are a perfect example of who I wish to reach. You do not embrace angry energy when it is cast in your direction. And like you, few others find comfort in it either. So I chose to take the gentle, understanding path of kind words. I prefer to share what I think would benefit most of those that would hear my words. You need not be concerned that my words will disrupt or dislodge souls around you. I am using you, a common man, because you are the epitome of those I wish to reach.

Scott, I wish to share the value of connection that one can experience on a personal level with energy such as mine.

So Jesus, is that the message?

It is one of them.

You do not have to be concerned about delivering a sermon that suggests ill behavior will place one in an eternal dungeon. You, my friend, will just tell others that they can come to me directly and that I will be there to connect with. You will not have a script to follow. I will not demand obedient action to earn forgiveness. I will just ask you to share from your heart and tell what you know. I will give you direction and words.

Few think of me as being that easy to be with. Do not think of yourself as a biblical leader. That is not your mission. There are many would-be leaders of biblical teachings that do not quite have it right. Not that they intend to be wrong. These leaders are teaching what is true for them. It would be more accurate to say that they have been misinformed.

The teachings of humanity have followed a course much like a childhood game that you played. You and your friends would sit in a circle and the first person whispers a word in the next person's ear. That action continues around the circle until the whispered word returns back to the first person. The object of the game was for the same word to reach all ears in the same circle with the same meaning and return to the first sender.

That typically does not happen. There is distortion between each sender and each receiver. So as the original word is sent through subsequent minds with different perceptions, the original words get changed as they are translated from mind to mind. The end result is that the last ear does not receive the same words with the same meaning that the first person sent out. Religious teachings are the same way. The teachings of the day that you might embrace are well meaning, but do not carry the original, intended energy that was embedded in the message long ago. Even tales of lore become changed and manipulated, depending on the intention of the teller. Do you see how this distortion transforms actual meanings?

Your own life is a perfect example. The rules of the day when you were growing up are not necessarily the rules that would apply to your world today. The messages you received from your parents are not totally relevant to your life now. So you can see my frustration in making sure the correct words arrive. That is where you come in. You can be the 'spell-check' in my narrative. You can bring the complexities of less-than-correct teachings to a simple, more palatable rendition.

This thing of life and living and ways to live by does not have to be hard. It is supposed to be easy.

Let me make this easy for you to understand. You are not expected to portray yourself as a fortune teller or a spiritual guide. I simply want you to relay my words to those who are willing to hear them. They are already hearing my words. They just do not know it. You are aware that I come to you. I come to many others, also. They just do not know it yet and it would be my preference that they did.

You are aware when I show up and embrace the connection. You have given yourself permission to meet with me and you do not allow yourself to feel unentitled. I want others to embrace the connection that awaits them. No credentials are needed to gain access to my energy and everyone can know that I am accessible.

Most are unaware of the one-to-one they can have with me and they do not realize that they have asked for it. Many feel undeserving and do not feel good enough to share in a conversation. They do not realize that I am like the neighbor down the street. It is not necessary to be anointed to have a sit-down. I am available 24/7. And I do not charge for the session.

You, on the other hand, believe in me because you have seen and heard me. You know that I am there and that has touched you to know that you can perceive my presence. On the occasions we have met, you willingly allowed me into your heart and simply enjoyed the experience. It is a simple process, would you not say? I knock on your energetic door and you say, "Come in," and we connect. It is a process that anyone who wants can be part of. There is plenty of me to go around.

Perceive me as an electrical generating station. Generators produce electricity the entire time, whether or not the power is being used. Sometimes there is more demand for a generator's electricity than other times. But they just keep generating for anyone to draw on at any moment.

My energy is strong enough for all to access. I come with power in hand to reach out to any asking soul. You cannot drain me and you cannot overload my circuits.

Sir, what about other religions where your name wouldn't hold much significance? When a follower of another religion calls on a counterpart of yourself who shows up to them? Is it you in disguise? Or are there others such as you that handle the other markets, so to speak.

Scott, there is a division of sorts that takes place. Other religions that exist in your world are counterparts of the religion you were raised in. At the head of any religion, there is a figurehead that is the central focus of the belief structure being proclaimed. It can be a mouse or a person or an imaginary being.

In all cases, however, there is a central core energy being tapped into. That is the same central core for all religions. It is important to know that any follower of any belief can access the central core of the philosophy they follow, just as I am instructing you and others to access me. There is no limit to the amount of connection that can be had. And it is individualized. No group counseling is necessary.

Whether you choose to realize it or not, all belief structures are funded with the same energy. That is to say, that the energy that keeps any belief structure in place is operating in the same universe as all other structures. There is no division of universes in place.

You are in and operate on the same energy that is moving any other belief system.

Scott, do you see what that means? That means that any belief system created or proclaimed has the same energy flowing through it. None are different energetically. No belief system is better than another. The difference only takes place on the human level. Humans create divisions in belief systems that are unnecessary. If the same energy is supporting all belief systems, then all belief systems are perfectly placed to operate on any level they wish. The systems do not collide except on a human, mental level. All beliefs are in perfect placement and deserve the same reverence and respect. So each soul should be at peace with who they are and know that they have a place in the universe to call their own. That stands for any soul or any belief structure. There is purpose and motive to each life.

Scott, would you care to ask additional questions?

Sir, I thought you'd never ask. How many do I get to throw at you?

It depends on how long you want this book to be.

I don't know where to start. There's so much I'd like to get your perspective on.

Scott, I will roll up my sleeves and we may begin.

Okay, let me start here. As I go through my day, I do query the universe a lot and I do get immediate answers. Then sometimes when I ask, I get what I'd call a watered-down response. It's sometimes the kind of response I'd expect from a politician, in that my question is sidestepped and even ignored. Or the answer is ambiguous. I don't understand that because there are the home run answers that I do get. Why aren't all answers definitive and direct? I don't understand the variance in the replies.

Scott, the variance is explainable this way. The nature of the question is the determining factor in the answers you get. The universe has a job to do and that is to create expansion on all levels.

If you pose a question where a direct answer would limit your expansion, the universe is less likely to respond categorically. It would be like someone doing your homework for you. If the universe were to answer you definitively on all levels, then there would be no need for you to explore the forest, as it were. There would be no learning situations that promote personal growth taking place. Do you see? When you ask a question from a perspective of personal growth, you are less likely to receive a definitive answer because the universe might see that you would benefit more from going through an experience personally rather than being told about it. Or the answer to your question is right around the corner in your life and is about to be addressed in an experiential sense. Does that answer feel right?

Yes, that resonates with me. At first, I wasn't sure how to take your answer, but as I tune in to how I feel, I'd have to say that it feels right. I'm not in any discord about it. I can see your point about benefitting from doing my own homework. It would have to be a better learning experience for me, instead of someone giving me the answer. The lesson or learning tends to stick better when one goes through it firsthand. But sometimes I just get lazy and want to read the ending of the book.

Exactly, Scott. That is simple universal understanding and it applies on all levels.

That is not to say that questions of a personal nature are not respected and ignored. You have to realize that the universe always hears you and just because you do not get an immediate answer, it does not mean the universe is not on task.

Your answer might be forthcoming experientially through contact with another person or event. You might receive an answer to a question from talking to a tree. By the way, that is possible to do. You just don't know what the source or vehicle is going to be that is going to supply an answer.

Simply stay vigilant and anticipate the arrival of the answer you are looking for. It will come when the universe feels you are ready to receive it. Do you see? So do not be an impatient receiver; let the universe work its magic.

When immediate answers are not forthcoming, know that it is in your best interest or the universe would have responded quickly. Remember, if the answer you are looking for is not immediate, it is probably because there is something for you to perceive in respect to the situation.

As an example, let us say that you ask the universe about fire. The universe could respond with an emphatic oratory about fire to include, "Do not play with it." Or in a coy sense, the universe could create a ringside seat for you to encounter fire on a personal level. The personal encounter of fire would be more far-reaching in your experience than if the universe simply told you what it was like.

Does that make better sense? The universe gives you firsthand experience when it can. It will take every opportunity to give you a ringside seat. If the universe feels you are not going to benefit from sitting ringside, then it will be much more informative when questioned. Do you see?

Yes, I see. Thank you, I get it. I've played with fire more than once and have learned a lot of life lessons that way. Mostly from being impatient.

Sir, I have been wondering about the possibilities of this next question for a while. In a way, it doesn't seem plausible to wonder about this. From your vantage point of existence, with all that you must see and being called on to the extent you probably are, I have to ask. Do you ever get mad?

Scott, you would have to understand my frame of mind to get a true answer to that question. Yes, I do get mad. I get mad at being misinterpreted and misquoted. It happens quite frequently. I have not said a lot of the things others claim I have spoken. It has really gotten out of control. Saying that it has reached epidemic proportions would be putting it mildly. You were not expecting an answer like that were you, Scott?

Not really. I didn't know quite what to expect, but the question had been rolling around in my head.

Scott, if I were there in person, there would be a sermon or two about who I really am and what I have really said in the past. There are those that are accurate in their interpretation of who I am and then there are those that are in left field, as you say.

So, Jesus, what does being mad in your world look like? Do you ever have a day when you just hate everyone and feel like throwing lightning bolts around? Do you kick the dog when you get home at night, or do you verbally take your frustration out on someone? Maybe there are walls around that you have put your fist through? Have you ever just had it with someone that simply won't listen to anything you tell them?

I can see you smiling at my question.

I have never been asked a question like that. And I have been asked a lot. No, I have not hit the wall or kicked the dog. I do not get mad, as you say, at individuals or things. My anger is more in the form of a longing for humankind. My heart gets heavy, as you might say, as I watch those stumbling through physical existence when they do not have to. My anger, such as it is, consists of the tempered action of continually looking for ways of improving myself. I have to keep improving myself before I can help others improve, do you see?

I question my existence every day, as you do. It might surprise you to hear that. There is a process in place for me, as well. I am a stepping stone of sorts. There are levels of understanding that I aspire to. There are no final stopping points for any soul. Only achievement of greater understanding. There are realms within realms. It guarantees that one never becomes bored with existence. There is always the next attraction in the amusement park. Does that satisfy your inquiry?

Yes, for now. But give me a minute to let that response incubate in my head. I never really thought that you had any challenges, as it were. My perception of you is that you have it all together.

Having it all together is a relative term. Each level of understanding comes with its own set of challenges. You simply learn more inventive ways of viewing a given event. Your wisdom develops and your perspective deepens as you grow. Any level of understanding comes with such an opportunity. So know that opportunities of expansion grace my horizon continually, as they do yours.

What is your next question, Scott? I know you to have questions about questions.

I'd like to know who you are. I know you're Jesus or some would say the Christ energy or Christ consciousness. I perceive you as a single energy at this moment, but I suspect that's just to relate to me on a human level. It doesn't really matter, I guess, but I'm a little confused with what I'm really connecting with when I have sessions like I'm having with you. So far in this narrative, I have connected with Gabe, my mother, grandfather, and a group unknown. As I meet these energies, they all seem different, but then I wonder if they are. I know I'm not on meds or schizophrenic, and that these encounters are real. But are they separate energies or connected? When I connect with you, which I enjoy by the way, are you singular Jesus or are you Gabe as well? Do I need to access individuals, as such, or is it all one ball of goo? Like a one-size-fits-all kind of thing.

Scott, you are wondering about connection points. It is truly interesting to me the depth of your thinking and need to know. Suffice it to say that I am the energy Jesus. You can come to me on that channel whenever you feel the need. I will comfort you the best I can when you stop in. I will guide you the best I know how without limiting your expansion and self-discovery. There are different energies all around you. They come and go as you come and go with daily encounters. Each of them is expanding as you are. Some days you will encounter equal energy and other days you might encounter energy that will make you stretch. You can even encounter lower energy, if you have that desire. You, however, do not attract that. You keep stretching. Your curiosity fuels you. So to more directly answer your question, I am singular, energetically. And Gabe is singular, energetically. He came to help as have I. He is me in a sense, but he is not. You are me, in a sense, but you are not. So for you to best utilize these connection points; continue to see them as singular when you call out to them. Sometimes you will not like the response, but they will always answer back.

So you're saying to keep doing what I'm doing. You're saying I should see the energies I connect with as singular but know that in some way they are all connected and to explore that would only confuse me. Is that right?

Yes, that would be a capsulated clarification. Let me add that you cannot expect direct answers all the time, but you can expect supportive connection all the time. Do you see that? Your frustration at times is because you get impatient and want solutions faster than they are forthcoming. You are continually being guided by caring energy even if you are not aware of it. Whether you want to call it a singular energy or group energy does not matter. It is there and it exists and you can perceive it in whatever form works best for you.

Scott, I can see that you are having trouble grasping what I just said. You are troubled by the phrase, 'caring energy' being around you all the time. You are struggling to associate something called caring energy around you and what that would look like. You want to attach an image and process to this something called caring energy. You want to be able to understand the process of how energy could be on tap to help you 24/7. You are trying to imagine what kind of an entity would be able and willing to constantly monitor your being and keep you on track.

Um, yes. You're right-on.

Humanly speaking, that would be a tall order. Think in terms of a spider web. In your world, when an insect lands on a web, the tending spider feels a change in the vibration of the web and knows how to respond.

Stop thinking in human terms. Your energy is part of a grid, like a spider web. You and every other person are plugged into this grid. Know that you are an energetic being. Just as a computer works without you knowing how it is working, the universe works as well. Yes, you are in a physical suit but you are all about energy from head to toe. The universe acts the same way. The cord that connects you to the universal spider web is energetically plugged in at all times. Your energy and everyone else's energy on the planet is sensed by the grid, like the spider tending its web. When there is any ripple in one's life, that energetic distortion is conveyed to the grid, and you are recognized and helped in whatever form the universe can muster.

Help might look like a neighbor's barking dog that gets your attention and causes you to check to see if someone is hurt and cannot call for help. After sensing the need, the universe sends help to the person needing it in the form of making the dog bark unusually, which gets your attention and causes you to see what is going on.

So for you, my friend, who has a need to know and wants a simple explanation on how everything in the universe works, that is as simple as it can be explained. If you prefer, you can see yourself attached to a long silver cord that stretches to any length and never gets unplugged. It is like the cord on your toaster, just a lot longer.

Thanks for explaining all that. It gives me another foothold. Sir, do you have time for another pondering?

Of course, I do.

I know that this is terribly human of me and I apologize in advance. Today nothing went right and it seemed that everyone I encountered throughout the day was difficult to work with. At one point, I got in my truck and wondered what the heck I'm doing this for. What is the reason to be here and keep plugging away on a road to nowhere, in a sense. At some point I'm going to run out of time and everything in my life will just have been an event. Someone will be able to carve on a stone, "He came, he saw, he left." What is the purpose to this physical life? A lot of the time, it's mundane repetition. Generally all of us on the planet fear the ultimate departure that we hope leads to another existence. So why are eight billion plus of us doing this thing called 'life'?

I want to think that there's a guardian angel on each shoulder and that there are angels under the wings of my plane holding me up in the air and that there's an all-knowing red dragon named Leroy who will sit with me on the moon. I want to think that there's a reason and a reward for doing what I do every day to keep the ship afloat. I'd hate to think that all that goes on in my day-to-day life is just so this physical body can maintain and exist until it can't. This is part of my need to know, of course.

Scott, there are angels on your shoulders and under your wings. And Leroy did sit with you on the moon.

Your last statement brought up a lot of emotion for me. I'm not sure just what I was getting emotional about, but thank you.

You are consumed with emotion from that realization. It struck you that you were actually in connection with realities bigger than you. You want to believe that bigger realities exist, but you are not totally convinced. You believe and share, but the skeptic in you still holds back 25% on the verification scale. Your heart was touched with realization on a level that you seldom experience. It was enjoyable for you to experience that depth of emotion. You normally work very hard to avoid that. You had a brush with your heart. That was heart energy at work.

Sir, you have me stuck here again. I'm not sure what to do with something called 'heart energy.'

You will. This was a defining moment for you and your heart was touched. There is no direct answer for you at this moment, but the answers will be forthcoming.

Scott, you fear life and you fear death, is that correct?

I don't think that's entirely right. I thoroughly enjoy the challenges of life and the adventure of achieving. When I'm not sure what to do, I try something just to see what happens. I never feel like I have a handle on things, however. I'm not sure I'm doing things right. I always thought I'd reach a point in my life where I'd have it all figured out and be on Easy Street. That hasn't happened and it's truly frustrating to me. What I fear the most is the end of it all. I'm afraid to run out of time. I don't know what that's going to look like and it's been a fear of mine since I was a small child. Maybe you're aware.

I feel your concerns and pain, and I want to assure you that there is purpose in every action that you take in any sense. This life is a stepping stone and is the amusement park you have spoken of. It is like the Ferris wheel in the center of the park. You have gotten on the big wheel to see what it is like to go high and go low and then go high again and see the view.

The view changes immensely, depending on your way up or down. Do you see how this equates with life? There are highs and lows that your days take you through and your vantage point on life changes depending on whether you are on an uphill trend or descending. Part of your experience is based on the attitude that you generate within. Seldom do you walk into an amusement park with the attitude of being sad and frustrated that you are there. You are generally upbeat upon your arrival. You cannot wait to get inside and go on the first ride. Then you get excited and cannot wait to go on to the next, and the next, and so on. Your life is just like that. You chose to come to this life and you were filled with excitement and expectation. You have been on many rides that take you up and down. The trick is to always be excited about the next attraction.

If you need to recover after an attraction, stop and sit on a bench along the way and eat a hot dog. Watch all the other people getting on and off the same rides you just experienced. Maybe go back and have another encounter with one of the rides you were already on. You have already purchased the ticket, so why not enjoy the event to your fullest?

There is no substitute for a great ride. And as a counterpart, there is no substitute for having a break in the action between the attractions. That is normal. There has to be the next low for there to be the next high. Do you see? So the turmoil of life that swings you into a questioning state should be welcomed with open arms because it is telling you that another exciting spin is on the way.

Jesus, I really like your analogy, but that doesn't explain why I bothered to come to the amusement park at all. That is, assuming I came from somewhere and was not just spawned on the spot to exist only to reach a termination point. Why plug the cord into the grid?

What I'd really like is for you to tell me something that justifies my existence. I want to hear why I should keep on doing what I do. Is there any point to this life? Sure there are amusements along the way, but in the end is it going to matter anyway?

Scott, you are bold and inventive yet you lack a sense of adventure in one sense. A true explorer does not ask why he is exploring, he just knows that he is looking to see what is over the next hill and is caught up in the adventure of the exploration. He does not know what he is going to find until he gets over the next hill. His whole being is geared to nothing else but experiencing the discovery of the yet unseen.

You were in existence before you came to the planet and you are going to exist after you finish your ride.

Then, Sir, I have to ask where is 'here' and why did I decide to leave and come to the park. What was my motivation?

There is a lot of motivation for you to take a trip such as you are on. The trip enriches your soul. It is a detour from the mundane that you experience in a perfect existence. Your adventures of the present are the rides in the amusement park for the soul of eternity. Each trip to the amusement park thrills the soul in a different way. There is no other reason to arrive where you are. You are where you are now, having come from where you were before. Where you were before does not really matter. All that matters is where you are now. Do you see? What matters is the exploring spirit. There is no benefit to dwelling on what might be or has been. It has no bearing on you now to be concerned about where you came from to get here or where you are going. You cannot really do anything about it anyway. You are going to go where you are going to go, whether you ponder it or not.

Consider being in the middle of a conversation with another person. Prior to the conversation, you may have planned on using words that did not get expressed and after the conversation, you consumed yourself with what you should have said. In the overall process of a conversation, you spend needless energy futurizing and then you spend needless energy dwelling on the past.

My wish for you in this moment is for you to utilize all of your energy to enjoy being, Scott. Do not get lost in the 'Scott' that was or might be. If you stay with the 'Scott' that exists in this very moment, you will not be in discord. Mental gyrations around what was and what might be can consume you, causing you to miss out on the experience of where you are in the immediate now.

Sir, being a practical type I see no reason to waste energy in any sense and I hadn't thought of mental grinding being a waste of energy until you pointed it out. So I'll start to consider that awareness in my ongoing moments as I enjoy who I am. I wasn't expecting this teaching but I can see the value in it.

So are you saying we arrive, we jump on a few rides and enjoy them the best we can, and then leave?

I can't see where it's that simple. It's frustrating to me to think that all the effort I've put into self-understanding is just a ride. Am I hearing you say there's no end zone to strive to reach or goal line to cross? That means there's no need to put out effort for some predisposed destination. That suggests no grand purpose to this life other than to experience. Do we just come to get on the big wheel and enjoy the view? That suggests we just keep dancing. Is that it?

Essentially, yes. Scott, are you disappointed?

I don't know. I always thought I was striving in some sense to elevate myself so that I'd get a blue ribbon at the end. Only to find out that there's no race. And there's no one there at the end handing out blue ribbons. What the hail?

I want there to be a grand design, as it were. I want there to be a reason to strive. I want to be the winner. Why should anyone strive to be a good person, whatever a 'good person' is? Why not just be a big jerk and mess with whomever you want to, in any way you want to, any time you want to.

Scott, there are big jerks doing what big jerks do. That is the experience they want to have and good for them, for knowing what they want to do. If you want to be a big jerk and hang out with the other big jerks, you can. And you will encounter the same consequences or experiences, if you will, that the other big jerks will experience as a result of the choice that they have made. Do you see how this works?

Your slate is blank. You can check the box that says, "I would like the experience of being a big jerk and all that goes with it," or you can check the box that says, "I would like the experience of finding out who I am and all the experience that goes with that, including passing on to others what I can to help them grow." Know that the box you checked will have its related consequences, just like checking the big jerk box. You could even check the box that says, "I know I have been a big jerk and I would like to experience how not to be one." So it all comes down to whether you want to check the box that has chocolate or the box that has vanilla. Each will release its related energy, and the two are not the same.

Scott, are you disappointed that you did not check the big jerk box?

No, I don't regret the box I've checked. It's been quite a ride to this point and I don't think the ride is over. I'm just trying to find something to believe in and everything you have been telling me makes sense but it hasn't given me a reason to keep on keeping on, if you know what I mean. My guess is that even big jerks get tired of what they're doing and wonder why they're here.

This attitude that I'm expressing has been reinforced lately, having uncovered some family secrets that I didn't know existed and I'm going through some disillusionment. Again, people in my life aren't who I thought they were or who they presented themselves to be.

I may be at the bottom of the Ferris wheel here and I don't mean to dispel your intent, but I still don't get where this life is taking me and what matters and what doesn't matter. I keep hoping you're going to hit the nail on the head for me here. What I've heard from you to this point seems rather ambiguous to me. I'm still looking for some hard and fast explanation of a way to justify my existence.

Let us take that last sentence where you say, 'justify my existence.' Scott, there is no existence to justify. There is only the act of living and the meaning you attach to it.

Jesus, that doesn't strike me as a good selling point to go around peddling to the masses. No one goes out and says to everyone, "Have fun. There's no real reason for you to be here. Have a nice day."

Scott, first of all, you will not be peddling to the masses. The masses are a tough crowd. You are going to touch the hearts of those who are ready for your words. I wish to iterate that many will not be able to hear the words you will offer. They will hear other words for now and that will be their calling. Do not discard them; they are where they need to be in the stepping stone process.

It sounds like what you're referring to is, "When the student is ready the teacher appears."

Yes, Scott, that is another way of putting it.

Okay so now, being the student, is the teacher ready to tell me and the remaining eight billion others on the planet categorically why we're here and what is the reason to push on?

There is no reason to push on unless you want to.

It feels like you're dodging my line of questioning. Are you saying that when you get right down to it, there's no meaning to life? I have to ask why you were here some 2,000 years ago. Really, what was the intention of that existence? And I ask that not with any intended disrespect because the same question would apply to my life. Why am I here now and will it matter at all in 2,000 years?

You ask a very heavy question and I hope to answer it with some clarity for you. The purpose of my life some 2,000 years ago was two-fold. First I wanted to accelerate a consciousness level – and I did. There were a lot of offshoots from that event. Some expected and some unanticipated but, never-the-less, minds were moved to another level. There were connections made that had never existed before and, as a result, man started to look at himself differently and consciously. He saw hope where he had not before. There were trials and tribulations generated from the event I partook of. But it freed a lot of hearts and caused them to open differently. Do you see? It was time for that to happen. The teacher appeared and the students who were ready took advantage of the teaching.

Second, what I gained from the experience was growth on an enormous level. I learned to love. It was a test for me. It was an extreme test, perhaps, in the eyes of onlookers. But also it tested me – who I was and who I became. While in the physical, I was unaware of the box I had checked and I doubted myself along the way. I wondered who I was and why I was so steadfastly determined to task myself with such an endeavor. Yet I was driven, as you are, to pursue and see what is over the next hill and understand who I am.

I am not asking you to duplicate my experience; there is no reason to unless you want to experience such a thing. I had to do what I did to test my strengths and weaknesses, as you do daily with your life experience. Do you see? It was simply a process I chose as a way of seeing who I really was and what I was capable of. It was the box I checked and chose to participate in.

Sir, that wouldn't be a ride I'd choose to get on.

A moment ago you said that man had hope, where he'd had none before. What hope did man gain from the experience of your life at that time?

I spoke of the same things then that I speak of now. You need to have hope of expansion. You have a world that is much more comfortable to live in now than long ago.

So Sir, there are eight billion souls on this planet testing themselves? What is the reason eight billion lives are in place on this planet? There has to be a simple way of explaining it. Am I asking about something that's a guarded secret?

You have every right to know what is going on. You are part of the whole situation. And you have asked so I will tell you. Humanity is an expansion point of the universe. There are many souls acting together. Simply put, there is no reason for any of the eight billion to be here unless they want the experience of understanding who they are and evolving to the next level. That is all there is to tell you. There is a process that each soul goes through to get to the physical, but none are denied. You and all the others wanted to come here to play and learn and find the limits of your expression.

Some play harder and get on more rides than others, and that is okay.

I want to impress on you that your experience in life is a direct result of the attitude you apply. If you arrive at the gate of the amusement park full of enthusiasm and excitement about what is about to take place, you are going to have a much different experience than if you buy your ticket feeling complacent and full of resistance. Just get on the ride and see what happens. Suffice it to say, you already bought your tickets. Invest in yourself and keep getting on the next ride.

You want to hear that everything will be alright. It will be. I cannot tell you what form of 'alright' will occur for you, but everything will be alright. Even if you voluntarily stopped functioning now and just sat down in your tracks and did nothing, everything would be okay. You would experience a set of conditions that you have not gone through before. That would be okay. After all, Scott, where you are now is a direct result of having sat down in the last set of tracks you left. Make a new set of prints. Go wild. Maybe do it with bare feet.

Sir, I truly hear what you're saying, however I'm missing the part where I'm supposed to get comfort from all of this. What you're telling me is hard fact, I assume. What I think I'm hearing is I chose and made my own bed, so I'm now sleeping in it. But I can choose to make another bed and sleep in that if I want to. I'd say that most readers wouldn't want to hear that. Generally I'm okay with hard fact and accept responsibility for my own life. I don't expect anyone to take care of me, but I'm human and I have my moments of wondering if we're having fun yet.

I'm looking for a button to push where all the lights go off and the confetti falls and the signs that says, "YOU CAN RELAX NOW," flashes on and off. I was hoping you could tell me where the button is. But you don't seem to be giving that up.

Sir, being a messenger at heart, I was hoping that while connecting with you I could receive firsthand the queen mother of inspirational thoughts that no one has heard from you before. I was hoping to get the pick of the litter of sage guidance. I wanted to connect with you and have you give me the best advice of all time that would comfort me and carry me to the end of my physical days in total bliss.

But no. All I'm getting is, "Paddle your own canoe."

So, sir, how did I do? Was that dramatic? Did I come across as needy and desperate?

Scott, it is certain that you missed a potential calling. It may serve you in your next life to try out the experience of creating dramatic fiction. That was a fine demonstration of situational frustration. However, I know you were partly serious.

There is much I could say here, but you always prefer the short version that may come across as harsh. I am not the fall guy here; I can help you and others if you seek me out. I can explain the roads that lay ahead but I cannot tell you where the roads will lead. I can only tell you that there is a road of sorts to your left and another on your right. I can present you with opportunity but it is up to you to travel it. I cannot make your life perfect; only you can do that. I can give you moral support until I am purple and I can supply you with 'Atta boys' and 'Atta girls' all day. But in the end you are the one who has to jump off the diving board into the pool. And you are the one that decides if you are going to swim on or simply float on your back.

I can be there when you come up for air and tell you it will be okay, and I have done that. After jumping in the pool, if it looks like you are having trouble getting to the surface, I can reach into the water and pull you up to the top. I have done that for you, too. I dearly love you and you have my total support. Do not feel I am slighting you by not giving you the answer you want to hear. I am giving you the only answers I have to give you. Anything else would be false instruction.

Scott, there is nothing up my sleeve. A primary theme I am trying to have you see is taking responsibility for your own life. No one else is going to set up your life so that you can relax. Not even me. That story of the powers that be having a plan for your life is highly overrated. You would do better with the story of trust few and paddle your own canoe. That sums up what I want to get across here. It goes to the story of give a man a fish and he will eat for a day, but if he learns to use a fishing pole he can eat every day. I know you have heard that one.

Scott, you can truly have fun paddling your own canoe if you CHOOSE TO. I enjoy our connection. I implore others to do the same. I am here to support any venue you choose to explore. I am your coach in all aspects you seek. If a set of actions is not working for you, then choose another. After choosing, do not get discouraged with your choice. Simply play it out for a while.

Scott, you are a messenger. Do not mess this up. Tell the stories that come to mind. Share your thoughts and ideas. Those that need to hear them will.

Let me leave you with these words and pass them on to others as well.

It is not possible to tell you how successful you will be in life. But I am here to tell you that you will not be disappointed with the results. Do not let insecure thoughts take hold of you. You are able to talk to the heavens. Your gift is here.

We love you and support you and we know that you are capable of loving yourself. We know that self-love is vital to a successful life. Success is relative to the endeavors you choose to challenge yourself.

If you develop self-love, that is the greatest gift you could give to yourself. Do not destroy your being by embellishing yourself with negative thoughts of non-achievement. There are many choices in the roads that one can travel. You get to choose. There are no wrong *turns. Just roads less traveled or heavily followed. You get to pick. Do not hesitate to choose one.*

Life will not choose for you. It will give you options to consider. Do not console yourself with excuses. There are no such things as excuses, only options not taken advantage of.

So in your new awareness of who you are, be advised that this is not a token ride. It is a ride of epic proportions that has the opportunity of achieving grandeur. And why would you not want to achieve grandeur? I have given you plenty of ponderings to consider. Pick the ones that fit for you. When you grow tired of the current style, keep your eyes open for the new updated ones and then try on one of those.

Just one last thought, Scott. If, on a given morning, every living soul on the planet were to look into a mirror, you all would be looking at the God that gave you life, the God that has brought you to this point of existence, and the God that will be with you to fulfill your destiny.

Remember, in a sense, I live right down the street and I am looking forward to when we meet again. Do not hesitate to enter the worlds of fascination and possibilities. Be sure to log the adventures so that you can share with me when next we encounter.

So, Scott, how did I do? Do you get it yet?

Made in the USA
San Bernardino, CA
25 January 2019